PYTHON: LEARN HOW TO WRITE CODES

WRITE CODES

Your Perfect Step by Step Guide

By Ken Fisher

Table of Contents

CHAPTER ONE

INTRODUCTION

I initially needed to learn Python in light of the fact that I needed to make a computer diversion. I had taken a few programming classes in school (C, C++, and Java) however nothing truly genuine. I'm not a Computer Science major and I don't program on an expert level.

I didn't generally like the low-level work included with C/C++. Things like pointers, memory administration, and different ideas were troublesome for me to handle, considerably less adequately utilize. Java, as my first ace gramming class in school, didn't bode well. I had never utilized an item arranged language before and article situated programming (OOP) ideas gave me fits. It likely didn't help that my Java class wasn't really genuine Java; it was really Microsoft's "custom" rendition: J++. So not just was I taking in a language that had minimal reasonable utilization (J++ included and cut numerous components found in genuine Java), however the programs didn't work accurately. At last the class was canceled close to the end of the semester and everybody got full credit.

These issues, and issues learning other programming languages, left a terrible taste in my mouth for programming. I never thought I took in a language all around ok to feel good utilizing it, significantly less really appreciate programming. However, then I caught wind of Python on a PC gathering, and saw a few different notice of the language at different destinations around the Internet. Individuals were discussing how incredible the language was for individual undertakings and how adaptable it is. I chose to give programming one more attempt and check whether Python was the language for me.

To give me more motivation to take in the language, I chose to recreate a pretending diversion from my adolescence as a PC amusement. In addition to the fact that i would have motivation to take in the language at the same time, ideally, I would have something valuable that I could provide for others for their happiness.

1.1 Why Python?

Python is viewed just like an incredible specialist language, yet it is additionally a to a great degree effective language. It has ties for C/C++ and Java so it can be utilized to tie vast undertakings together or for fast prototyping. It has an implicit GUI (graphical client interface) library by means of Tkinter, which lets the programmer make straightforward graphical interfaces with little exertion. Notwithstanding, other, all the more capable and complete GUI developers are accessible, for example, Qt and GTK+. IronPython, a Python rendition for Windows utilizing the .NET structure, is likewise accessible for those utilizing Microsoft's Visual Studio items. Python can likewise be utilized as a part of a genuine time mediator for testing code pieces before including them into a typical "executable".

Python is named a scripting language. As a rule, this fair implies that it's not aggregated to make the machine-meaningful code and that the code is "tied-into" another program as a control schedule. Arranged languages, for example, C++, require the programmer to run the source code through a compiler before the product is can be utilized by a PC. Contingent upon the program's size, the accumulation procedure can take minutes to hours.

Utilizing Python as a control routine means Python can go about as a "paste" between distinctive programs. Case in point, Python is frequently utilized as the scripting language for feature recreations; while the substantial obligation work is performed by precompiled modules, Python can act in a call/response design, for example, taking controller info and passing it to the fitting module.

Python is likewise viewed as an abnormal state language, importance it deals with a considerable measure of the snort work included in programming. For instance, Python has an implicit trash specialist so you, as a programmer, don't generally need to stress over memory administration and memory releases, a typical event when utilizing more seasoned languages, for example, C.

The primary accentuation of Python is decipherable code and upgrading star grammer profitability. This is expert by authorizing a strict method for organizing the code to guarantee the peruser can take after the rationale stream and by having an "everything's incorporated" mindset; the programmer doesn't need to stress over including many libraries or other source code to make his program work.

One of the fundamental contentions against Python is the utilization of whitespace. As indicated in Chapter 3, numerous different languages require the programmer to utilize sections, normally wavy supports, i.e. "{}", to distinguish diverse squares of code. With Python, these code pieces are distinguished by different measures of space.

Individuals who have invested a great deal of energy with "customary" languages feel the absence of sections is a terrible thing, while others lean toward the white space. Eventually, it boils down to individual inclination. I happen to like the absence of sections on the grounds that its one less thing I need to investigate when there is a coding issue. Envision that one missing section in a few dozen to hundreds lines of code is the reason your program won't work. Presently envision needing to experience your code line by line to locate the missing section. (Yes, programming situations can help yet it's still one additional thing to consider).

1.2   Why Another Tutorial?

Despite the fact that there are a few extraordinary instructional exercises at the Python site((http://www.python.org), notwithstanding numerous books, my accentuation will be on the down to earth components of the language, i.e. I won't go into the historical backdrop of the language or the elusive ways it can be utilized. In spite of the fact that it will help in the event that you have programmed some time recently, or possibly can comprehend programming rationale and program stream, I will attempt to verify that things begin moderate so you don't get befuddled.

The principle motivation behind this book is to show individuals how to program; Python just happens to be the language I have decided to utilize. As said above, it is an inviting language which gives you a chance to figure out how to program without getting in your direction. The vast majority, when they choose to learn programming, need to hop into C, C++, or Java. Notwithstanding, these languages have little "gotchas" that can make taking in troublesome and deter individuals from proceeding with programming. My

Objective is to present programming in a fun, neighborly way so you will have the yearning to take in more.

1.3   Getting Python

As of this modification, Python 3.x has been out for quite a while. The greater part of my experience is with Python 2.4 and 2.5, however a lot of my insight was picked up from perusing books composed for adaptation 2.2. As should be obvious, it doesn't fundamentally mean your insight is old when another form turns out. Generally the fresher forms essentially include new elements, frequently includes that a learner won't have a requirement for.

Python 3.x breaks similarity with programs written in 2.x versions. Notwithstanding, a significant part of the learning you pick up from taking in a 2.x rendition will in any case persist. It just means you must be mindful of the progressions to the language when you begin utilizing form 3.0. Furthermore, the introduce base of 2.x is huge and won't be going ceaselessly for a long while. Because of the way that most Linux dispersions (and Mac OS X) still have more seasoned Python adaptations introduced naturally (some as old as v2.4), large portions of the code samples in this book are composed for Python

2.x. Uncommon note is rolled out of noteworthy improvements somewhere around 2.x and 3.x in the part around 19, yet adapting either form won't hurt you.

You can download Python from the Python site((for Windows) or it might as of now be introduced on your system in case you're utilizing a Mac, Linux, or *BSD. Be that as it may, the Unix-like operating systems, including OS X, might not have the most recent form so you may wish to update, at any rate to form 2.6. Rendition 2.6 is an adjustment of 2.5 that permits utilization of both 2.x code and certain 3.0 capacities. Basically it gives you a chance to code in "legacy" style while as yet having the capacity to utilize the most recent elements as fancied, and testing which legacy components will be broken when moving to 3.0.

For those keen on utilizing Python by means of a USB thumbdrive, you may be occupied with Portable Python. This is an independent Python environment that you can either keep running from the thumbdrive or introduce to your PC. This is valuable for individuals who can't or would prefer not to introduce Python yet might in any case want to utilize it.

I'll expect you can make sense of how to get the

intuitive mediator running; in the event that you need help, read the help pages on the site. Generassociate talking however, you open up summon incite (or terminal) and sort "python" at the brief. This will open a Python session, permitting you to work with the Python mediator in an intuitive way. In Windows, ordinarily you simply go to the Python document in All Programs and snap it.

1.4   Conventions Used in this Book

The most recent adaptation of Python is 3.2 while the most current "legacy" variant is 2.7. I will utilize the term 3.x to connote anything in the Python 3 family and 2.x for anything in the Python 2 family, unless expressly expressed.

The expression "*nix" is utilized to allude to any Unix-like language, including Linux and the different kinds of BSD (FreeBSD, OpenBSD, NetBSD). Despite the fact that Mac OS X is based upon FreeBSD, it is sufficiently distinctive to not be lumped in the *nix mark.

Because of the word-wrap organizing for this book,

a few lines are consequently indented when they are truly on the same line. It may make a portion of the cases befuddling, particularly in light of the fact that Python uses "white space" like tabs and spaces as huge zones. Therefore, a word- wrapped line may have all the earmarks of being an indented line when it truly isn't. Ideally you will have the capacity to make sense of if a line is deliberately tabbed over or essentially wrapped.

CHAPTER TWO

HOW IS PYTHON DIFFERENT?

So what is Python? Chances you are asking yourself this. You may have discovered this book on the grounds that you need to figure out how to program yet don't know anything about programming languages. Then again you may have known about programming languages like C, C++, C#, or Java and need to realize what Python is and how it contrasts with "huge name" languages. Ideally I can clarify it for you.

2.1   Python Concepts

In the event that you're not inspired by the hows and whys of Python, don't hesitate to skip to the following part. In this section I will attempt to disclose to the peruser why I think Python is one of the best languages accessible and why it's an awesome one to begin programming with.

2.1.1 Dynamic versus Static Types

Python is an element wrote language. Numerous different languages are static written, for example, C/C++ and Java. A static wrote language requires the programmer to expressly tell the PC what kind of "thing" every information quality is. Case in point, in the on the off chance that you had a variable that was to contain the cost of something, you would need to proclaim the variable as a "buoy" sort. This tells the compiler that the main information that can be utilized for that variable must be a gliding point number, i.e. a number with a decimal point. In the event that some other information worth was relegated to that variable, the compiler would give a slip when attempting to incorporate the program.

Python, be that as it may, doesn't oblige this. You just give your variables names and relegate qualities to them. The mediator deals with staying informed regarding what sorts of items your program is utilizing. This likewise implies that you can change the extent of the qualities as you add to the program. Let's assume you have another decimal number (a.k.a. a coasting point number) you require in your program. With a static wrote language, you need to choose the memory measure the variable can take when you first instate that variable. A twofold is a gliding point esteem that can deal with a much bigger number than a typical buoy (the genuine memory sizes rely on upon the operating environment). In the event that you proclaim a variable to be a buoy yet later on relegate an esteem that is too huge to it, your program will fall flat; you will need to backtrack and change that variable to be a twofold.

With Python, it doesn't make a difference. You essentially give it whatever number you need and Python will deal with controlling it as required. It even works for inferred qualities. Case in point, say you are isolating two numbers. One is a drifting point number and one is a number. Python understands that its more precise to stay informed regarding decimals so it naturally computes the outcome as a gliding point number. This is what it would look like in the Python mediator.

```
>>>6.0 / 2
```

3 . 0

```
>>>6 / 2 . 0
```

3 . 0

As should be obvious, it doesn't make a difference which esteem is on top or base; Python "sees" that a buoy is being utilized and gives the yield as a decimal quality.

2.1.2 Interpreted versus Incorporated

Numerous "conventional" languages are arranged, significance the source code the designer composes is changed over into machine language by the compiler. Ordered languages are normally utilized for low-level programming (for example, gadget drivers and other equipment connection) and speedier professional cessing, e.g. feature diversions.

Since the language is preconverted to machine code, it can be prepared by the PC much faster on the grounds that the compiler has effectively checked the code for blunders and different issues that can bring about the program to fall flat. The compiler won't get all blunders however it does help. The proviso to utilizing a compiler is that aggregating can be a period expending undertaking; the genuine assembling time can take a few minutes to hours to finish contingent upon the program. In the event that mistakes are found, the designer needs to discover and fix them then rerun the compiler; this cycle proceeds until the program meets expectations effectively.

Python is viewed as a translated language. It doesn't have a compiler; the translator forms the code line by line and makes a bytecode. Bytecode is in the middle of "language" that isn't exactly machine code yet it isn't the source code. In view of this in the middle of state, bytecode is more transferable between operating systems than machine code; this helps Python be cross-stage. Java is another language that uses bytecodes.

On the other hand, in light of the fact that Python utilizes a mediator as opposed to compiler, the code handling can be slower. The bytecode still must be "deci- phered" for utilization by the processor, which takes extra time. Yet, the advantage to this is that the programmer can instantly see the consequences of his code. He doesn't need to sit tight for the compiler to choose if there is a linguistic structure slip some place that causes the program to crash.

2.1.3 Prototyping

Due to understanding, Python and comparable languages are utilized for fast application advancement and program prototyping. Case in point, a basic program can be made in only a couple of hours and demonstrated to a client in the same visit.

Programmers can over and over change the program and see the results rapidly. This permits them to attempt distinctive thoughts and see which one is best without contributing a great deal of time on deadlocks. This additionally applies to making graphical client interfaces (GUIs). Straightforward "representations" can be laid out in minutes in light of the fact that Python has a few diverse GUI libraries accessible as well as incorporates a basic library (Tkinter) naturally.

Another advantage of not having a compiler is that lapses are immediately created by the Python mediator. Contingent upon the creating environment, it will naturally read through your code as you create it and advise you of linguistic structure blunders. Rationale slips won't be called attention to yet a straightforward mouse snap will dispatch the program and demonstrate to you last item. In the case of something isn't correct, you can just roll out an improvement and snap the dispatch catch once more.

2.1.4 Procedural versus Item Oriented Programming

Python is to some degree interesting in that you have two decisions when developing your programs: procedural programming or item situated. In actuality, you can blend the two in the same program.

Quickly, procedural programming is an orderly procedure of developing the program in a fairly direct mold. Capacities (now and again called subroutines) are called by the program on occasion to perform some preparing, and then control is returned back to the fundamental program. C and BASIC are procedural languages.

Article arranged programming (OOP) is only that: programming with items. Articles are made by unmistakable units of programming rationale; variables and systems (an OOP expression for capacities) are combined into items that do a specific thing. For instance, you could show a robot and every body part would be a different item, fit for doing distinctive things yet some piece of the general article. OOP is additionally vigorously utilized as a part of GUI improvement.

Actually, I feel procedural programming is simpler to learn, especially at first. The perspective is for the most part clear and basically direct. I never comprehended OOP until I began learning Python; it can be a troublesome thing to wrap your head around, especially when you are as yet making sense of how to get your program to function in any case.

Procedural programming and OOP will be talked about in more profundity later in the book. Every will get their own parts and ideally you will perceive how they expand upon natural ideas.

CHAPTER THREE

COMPARISON OF PROGRAMMING LANGUAGES

For the new programmer, a portion of the terms in this book will likely be new. You ought to have a superior thought of them when you wrap up this book. Be that as it may, you might likewise be new to the different programming languages that exist. This part will show a percentage of the more prevalent languages at present utilized by programmers. These programs are intended to show how every language can be utilized to make the same yield. You'll see that the Python program is altogether easier than the others.

The accompanying code samples all show the tune, "99 Bottles of Beer on the Wall" (they have been reformatted to fit the pages). You can discover more at the authority 99 Bottles site: http://99-containers   of-beer.net. I can't vouch that each of these programs is substantial and will really run accurately, yet in any event you get a thought of how everyone looks. You ought to additionally understand that, as a rule, white space is not critical to a programming language (Python being one of only a handful couple of special cases). That implies that the greater part of the programs underneath could be composed one line, put into one gigantic section, or some other blend. This is the reason a few individuals despise Python in light of the fact that it compels them to have organized, comprehensible code.

3.1   C

```
/*
 * 99bottles  of beerinansic
 *
 *byBill Wein: bearheart@bearnet.com
 *
 */
#defineMAXBEER(99)
```

```
voidchug(intbeers);
main()
{
registerbeers;
for(beers =MAXBEER; beers ;
    chug(beers--))puts("");
puts("\nTimetobuymore-
beer!\n");exit(0);
}
voidchug(registerbeers)
{
char howmany[8], *s;
s = beers !=1 ? "s" : "";
printf ("%dbottle%sof beeronthewall,\n", beers
    , s);
printf("%dbottle%sof beeeeer . . . ,\n", beers,s);
printf("Takeonedown, passit around,\n");
if(--beers) sprintf(howmany, "%d", beers); else
    strcpy(howmany,
"Nomore");s = beers !=1
? "s" : "";
printf("%sbottle%sof beeronthewall .\n" ,how-
    many, s);
}
```

3.2   C++

*//C++ version of 99Bottles of Beer,
    objectoriented paradigm*

25

```cpp
//programmer: TimRobinsontimtroyr@ionet.
NET
#include<fstream.h>
enumBottle { BeerBottle};
classShelf {
    unsigned BottlesLeft;
public:
    Shelf( unsigned bottlesbought )
        : BottlesLeft( bottlesbought )
        {}
    voidTakeOneDown()
        {
        if (!BottlesLeft)
    throw BeerBottle;BottlesLeft--;
        }
    operatorint() { returnBottlesLeft; }
    };

intmain( int, char**)
    {
    Shelf Beer(99);
    try{
        for(;;) {
            char*plural = (int)Beer!=1? "s"
                : "";
            cout<<(int)Beer<<" bot-
                tle"<<plural
```

```
                    <<" of beeronthewall,"<<endl
;
            cout<<(int)Beer<<" bottle"<<
                plural
                <<" of
            beer,"<<endl;Beer.
            TakeOneDown();
            cout<<"Takeonedown, passit around
                ,"<<endl;
            plural = (int)Beer!=1?
            "s":"";cout<<(int)Beer<<"
            bottle"<<
                plural
                <<" of beeronthewall ."<<endl
;
            }
        }
    catch( Bottle ) {
        cout<<"Gotothestore andbuysomemore
            ,"<<endl;
        cout<<"99bottles of beeronthewall."
            <<endl;
    }
    return0;
    }
```

1.3 Java

```
/**
* Java5.0 version of thefamous"99bottles of
    beeronthewall".
*Notetheuseof specific Java5.0 features and
    thestrictly correct output.
*
*@authorkvols
*/
importjava.util.*;
classVerse{
    privatefinal intcount;Verse(intverse)
    {count=100-verse;
    }
    publicString toString () {
        String c=
            "{0,choice,0#nomorebottles|1#1
                bottle|1<{0}bottles} of beer";
        returnjava.text.MessageFormat.format(
            c.replace("n","N")+"onthewall,
                "+c+".\n"+
            "{0,choice,0#Go tothestore
                andbuysomemore"+
            "|0<Takeonedownandpas-
                sit around},"+c.re-
                place("{0","{1")+
            " onthewall.\n", count, (count+99)
                %100);
```

```
        }
}
class Song implements Iterator<Verse>{
        private int verse=1;
        public boolean hasNext(){
                return verse <=100;
        }
        public Verse next(){
                if(!hasNext())
                        throw new NoSuchElementEx-
                            ception("End of song!");
                return new Verse(verse++);
        }
        public void remove() {
                throw new UnsupportedOpera-
                    tionException("Cannot rem-
                    ove verses!");
        }
}

        public class Beer{
                public static void
                    main(String[] args) {Iter-
                    able<Verse> song=new Iterable<
        Verse>(){
                        public Iterator<Verse>iterator()
        {
                                return new Song();
                        }
                };
```

```
//Allthis worktoutilize
    thisfeature:
//"Foreachverse inthesong..."
for(Verseverse : song)
    {System.out.printl-
    n(verse);

    }

  }

}
```

1.4 C#

```
///Implementationof Ninety–NineBottles
   of BeerSonginC#.
///What's  neatis that.NETmakestheBinge-
   classa full–fledged componentthatmaybe-
   calledfromanyother  .NETcomponent.
///
///PaulM.Parks
///http://www.parkscomputing.com/
///February8, 2002
///
usingSystem;
namespace NinetyNineBottles
{
    ///<summary>
    ///References themethodof output.
    ///</summary>
```

publicdelegate **void**Writer(string for-mat,paramsobject[] arg);

///<summary>

///References thecorrective action totakewhenwerun out.

///</summary>

publicdelegate **int**MakeRun();

///<summary>

///Theactof consumingall those beverages.

///</summary>

publicclassBinge

{

    ///<summary>

    ///Whatwe'll bedrinking.

    ///</summary>

    privatestring beverage;

    ///<summary>

    ///Thestarting count.

    ///</summary>

    privateintcount= 0;

    ///<summary>

    ///Themannerinwhichthelyrics are-output.

    ///</summary>

    privateWriterSing;

    ///<summary>

```
///Whattodowhenit's all gone.
///</summary>
privateMakeRunRiskDUI;
publiceventMakeRunOutOfBottles;
///<summary>
///Initializes thebinge.
///</summary>
///<paramname="count">Howmany
    we'reconsuming.
///</param>
///<paramname="disasterWaiting-
ToHappen">
///Ourinstructions, should wesucceed.
///</param>
///<paramname="writer">How
    ourdrinkingsongwill be-
    heard.</param>
///<paramname="beverage">What
    todrinkduringthis binge.</
    param>
publicBinge(string beverage, int-
    count,Writerwriter)
{
    this.beverage=beverage;
    this.count=count;
    this.Sing= writer;
}
///<summary>
///Let's getstarted.
```

```
///</summary>
publicvoidStart()
{
    while(count>0)
    {
        Sing(
@"
{0}bottle{1}of {2}on-
thewall,
{0}bottle{1}of {2}.
Takeonedown, passit around,",
                count, (count==1)
                    ? "": "s", beverage);


count--;

        if (count>0)
        {

}
    else
Sing("{0}bottle{1}of {2}onthewall.",
    count, (count==1)
        ? "": "s", beverage);
                {
                    Sing("No morebottles of
                    {0}onthewall.",bev-
                        erage, null);
```

```
            }
        }
        Sing(
            @"
    Nomorebottles of {0}onthewall,
    Nomorebottles of {0}.", beverage, null);

            if (this.OutOfBottles!=null)
            {
}
    else
{
}
  }
    }


count=this.OutOfBottles();
Sing("{0}bottles of  {1}on
    thewall.", count, beverage);

Sing("First weweep,  thenwesleep
    .");
Sing("No morebottles of {0}onthewall.",
    beverage,  null);
    ///<summary>
    ///Thesongremainsthesame.
    ///</summary>
```

```
class SingTheSong
{
    ///<summary>
    ///Any other numberwouldbestrange.
    ///</summary>
    const int bottleCount= 99;
    ///<summary>
    ///Theentrypoint. Setsthepa-
        rametersof theBingeand-
        starts it.
    ///</summary>
    ///<paramname="args">unused</
    param>
    static void Main(string[] args)
    {
        Binge binge=
            new Binge("beer",bottle-
            Count,
            new Writer(Console.
        WriteLine));binge.OutOfBot-
        tles+=new MakeRun(
            SevenEleven);binge.Start();
    }


    ///<summary>
    ///There's boundtobeonenearby.
    ///</summary>
    ///<returns>Whateverwould-
        fit inthetrunk.</returns>
```

```
static intSevenEleven()
{
    Console.WriteLine("Gotothe-
        store,getsomemore...");
    returnbottleCount;
}
    }
}
```

1.5 Python

```
#!/usr/bin/envpython
#-*-coding: iso-8859-1-*-
""""

99Bottles of Beer(byGeroldPenz)
Pythoncanbesimple, too:-)
""""

forquantinrange(99, 0, -1):
    if  quant>1:
        print(quant, "bottles of beeronthewall
            ,", quant, "bottles of beer.")
        if  quant>2:
            suffix = str(quant- 1) + " bottles
                ofbeeronthewall."
    else:
        suffix ="1 bottle of beeronthewall."
    elif quant==1:
```

```
print"1 bottle   of beer on the wall,
    1 bottle of beer."
suffix ="no more beer on the wall!"
print"Take one down, pass it around,", suffix
print"--"
```

CHAPTER FOUR

THE PYTHON INTERPRETER

4.1 Launching the Python interpreter

Python can be programmed by means of the intelligent summon line (otherwise known as the mediator or IDE) yet anything you code won't be spared. When you close the session it all goes away. To spare your program, its simplest to simply sort it in a content record and spare it (make certain to utilize the .py expansion, i.e. foo.py)

To utilize the mediator, sort "python" at the charge brief (*nix and Mac) or dispatch the Python IDE (Windows and Mac). In case you're utilizing Windows and introduced the Python .msi document, you ought to have the capacity to additionally sort Python on the charge brief. The principle distinction between the IDE and the charge brief is the summon brief is a piece of the operating system while the IDE is a piece of Python. The summon brief can be utilized for different assignments other than disturbing Python; the IDE must be utilized for Python. Use whichever you're more OK with.

In case you're utilizing Linux, BSD, or another *nix operating system, I'll accept you mechanically sufficiently slanted to think about the terminal; you presumably even know how to get Python up and running as of now. For the individuals why should utilized opening Terminal or Command Prompt (same thing, distinctive name on diverse operating systems), here's the means by which to do it.

4.1.1 Windows

1. Open the Start menu.

2. Click on "Run. . . "

3. Type "cmd" in the content box (without the quotes) and hit Return.

4. You ought to now have a dark window with white content. This is the charge brief.

5. If you write "python" at the brief, you ought to be dropped into the Python translator brief.

4.1.2 Mac

1. Open Applications

2. Open Utilities

3. Scroll down and open Terminal

4. You ought to have a comparative window as Windows clients above.

5. Type "python" at the brief and you will be in the Python mediator.

Here is the thing that your terminal ought to look like now: Listing 4.1: Example Python mediator

Python 2 . 5 . 1 (r 251 : 5 4 8 6 3 , Jan 17 2008 , 1 9 : 3 5 : 1 7)

[GCC 4 . 0 . 1 (Apple Inc . b u i l d 5465)] on darwin Type " help " , " c o p y r i g h t " , " c r e d i t s " or " l i c e n s e " for more i n f o r m a t i o n .

>>>

You may see that the Python variant utilized as a part of the above cases is 2.5.1; the present rendition is 3.2. Try not to frenzy. The dominant part of what you will realize will work paying little heed to what rendition you're utilizing. My most loved Python book, Python How to Program, is in view of form 2.2 yet regardless I utilize it almost consistently as a source of perspective while coding.

Generally, you won't even notice what adaptation is being used, unless you are utilizing a library, capacity, or system for a particular version. At that point, you basically add a checker to your code to distinguish what rendition the client has and advise him to redesign or adjust your code so it is in reverse good.

(A later section in this book will cover all the real contrasts you should be mindful of when utilizing Python 3.x. At this time you're simply taking in the essentials that you will utilize paying little respect to which form of the language you wind up utilizing.)

The >>> in Listing 4.1 is the Python order incite; your code is written here and the outcome is imprinted on the accompanying line, without a brief. Case in point, Listing 4.2 demonstrates a basic print articulation from Python 2.5:

Posting 4.2: Python charge brief

>>>print "We will be the k n i g h t s who say, " Ni " . " We are the knights who say , " Ni " .

4.2   Python Versions

As an aside, Python 3.x has changed print from a straightforward explanation, such as Listing 4.2, into a real capacity (Listing 4.3). Since we haven't discussed capacities yet, everything you need to know is that Python

3.x just obliges you to utilize the print proclamation in a marginally diverse manner: bracket need to encompass the cited words. So hopefully you're mindful.

Posting 4.3: Print capacity (Python 3.x)

```
>>>print ( "We will be the k n i g h t s who say,
" Ni " . " ) We are the k n i g h t s who say, " Ni ".
```

The larger part of the code in this book will be composed for Python 2.6 or prior, since those forms are introduced naturally on numerous *nix systems and is along these lines still extremely prominent; there is likewise a considerable measure of more established code in the wild, particularly open-source programs, that haven't been (and likely never will be) moved up to Python 3.x. In the event that you choose to utilize other Python programs to study from or use, you will need to know the "old school" method for Python programming; numerous open-source programs are still composed for Python 2.4.

On the off chance that you are utilizing Python 3.x and you need to sort each illustration into your PC as we come, please be mindful that the print proclamations, as composed, won't work. They will must be altered to utilize a print() capacity like in Listing 4.3.

4.3   Using the Python Command Prompt

On the off chance that you compose an announcement that doesn't oblige any "handling" by Python, it will essentially return you to the brief, anticipating your next or- der. The following code sample demonstrates the client doling out the quality "spam" to the variable can. Python doesn't need to do anything with this, as to figurings or anything, so it acknowledges the announcement and afterward sits tight for another articulation.

Posting 4.4: Python articulations

```
>>>can  = "spam"

>>>
```

(Incidentally, Python was named after Monty Python, not the snake. Henceforth, a great part of the code you'll discover on the Internet, instructional exercises, and books will have references to Monty Python portrays.)

The standard Python translator can be utilized to test thoughts before you place them in your code. This is a decent approach to hash out the rationale needed to make a specific capacity work effectively or perceive how a contingent circle will function. You can likewise utilize the mediator as a basic number cruncher. This may sound quirky, however I regularly dispatch a Python session for utilization as an adding machine on the grounds that its frequently quicker than navigating Windows' menus to utilize its number cruncher.

Here's an illustration of the "adding machine" capacities:

Listing 4.5: Python as a calculator

```
>>>2+2
4
>>>4*4
16
>>>5*2#five squared
 25
```

Python also has a math library that you can import to do trigonometric functions and many other higher mathematical calculations. Importing libraries will be covered later in this book.

4.4   Commenting Python

One last thing to examine is that remarks in Python are stamped with the "#" image. Remarks are utilized to clarify notes or other data without having Python attempt to perform an operation on them. Case in point,

Posting 4.6: Python remarks

>>>d i c t = {" F i r s t phonetic " : " Able", " Second phonetic " : " Baker"} #create a d i c t i o n a r y

>>>print d i c t . keys ( ) #d i c t i o n a r y values aren " t in request

[" Second phonetic " , " F i r s t phonetic "]

>>>print d i c t [" F i r s t phonetic "] #p r i n t the key " s esteem

Capable

You will see later on that, despite the fact that Python is an exceptionally decipherable language, regardless it serves to place remarks in your code here and there to expressly state what the code is doing, to clarify a perfect easy route you utilized, or to just help yourself to remember something while you're coding, similar to a "to-do" list.

4.5 Launching Python programs

In the event that you need to run a Python program, essentially sort python at the shell order brief (not the IDE or intuitive mediator) trailed by the program name.

Posting 4.7: Launching a Python program

$python foo . py

Records spared with the .py expansion are called modules and can be called exclusively at the summon line or inside of a program, like header documents in different languages. On the off chance that your program is going to import different modules, you will need to verify they are all spared in the same index on the PC. More data on living up to expectations with modules can be discovered later in this book or in the Python documentation.

Contingent upon the program, certain contentions can be added to the summon line when propelling the program. This is like adding changes to a Windows DOS brief charge. The contentions tell the program what precisely it ought to do. For instance, maybe you have a Python program that can yield its handled information to a record as opposed to the screen. To summon this capacity in the program you basically dispatch the program like so:

Posting 4.8: Launching a Python program with contentions

$python foo . py – f

The "-f" contention is gotten by the program and calls a capacity that prints the information to an assigned area inside of the PC's document system as opposed to printing it to the screen.

In the event that you have various variants of Python introduced on your PC, e.g. the system default is rendition 2.5 however you need to play around with Python 3.x, you basically need to advise the OS which form to utilize (see Listing 4.9). This is essential since numerous more established Python programs aren't promptly good with Python 3.x. As a rule, a more seasoned form of Python must be held on a PC to empower certain programs to run effectively; you would prefer not to totally overwrite more established Python renditions.

Posting 4.9: Selecting a Python form

```
$python2.5 test.py #force use of Python 2.5
```

```
$python3.0 test.py #force use of Python 3.0
```

4.6   Integrated Development Environments

I ought to take the time now to clarify all the more about programming environments. All through this book, the majority of the samples include utilizing the Python intelligent translator, which is utilized by writing "python" at the operating system order brief. This environment is truly more for testing thoughts or basic "one-shot" assignments. Since the information isn't put away anyplace, when the Python session is done, all the information you worked with goes away.

To make a reusable program, you have to utilize a source code proofreader. These editors can be a real programming environment application, a.k.a. IDEs (coordinated advancement situations), or they can be a basic content tool like Windows Notepad. There is nothing unique about source code; paying little mind to the programming language, it is just content. IDEs are fundamentally improved word processors that give exceptional apparatuses to make programming less demanding and faster.

Python has numerous IDEs accessible and almost every one of them are free. Regularly, an IDE incorporates a source code manager, a debugger, a compiler (a bit much for Python), and frequently a graphical client interface developer; distinctive IDEs may incorporate or evacuate certain elements. The following is a rundown of some normal Python IDEs:

- Eric-a free application that goes about as a front-end to different programs and uses modules

- IDLE-a free application included in the base Python establishment; incorporates a coordinated debugger

- Komodo-a full-included, restrictive application that can be utilized for other programming languages

- PyDev-a module for the Eclipse advancement environment

- Stani's Python Editor (SPE)-a free application that incorporates numerous improvements

TYPES AND OPERATORS

Python is in light of the C programming language and is composed in C, such a large amount of the arrangement Python uses will be recognizable to C and C++ programmers. In any case, it makes life a little less demanding on the grounds that it's not made to be a low-level language (its hard to connect vigorously with equipment or perform memory assignment) and it has fabricated in "refuse gathering" (it tracks references to questions and naturally expels objects from memory when they are no more referenced), which al- lows the programmer to stress all the more over how the program will function instead of managing the PC.

5.1 Python Syntax

5.1.1 Indentation

Python constrains the client to program in an organized configuration. Code squares are dictated by the measure of space utilized. As you'll review from the Comparison of Programming Languages section, sections and semicolons were utilized to show code gathering or end-of-line termicountry for alternate languages. Python doesn't require those; indentation is utilized to imply where every code square begins and finishes. Here is an illustration (line numbers are included for elucidation):

Posting 5.1: White space is critical

1. x = 1

2. if x : # if x i s t mourn

3. y = 2

4. if y : # if y i s t mourn

5. print " square 2 "

6. print " square 1 "

7. print " square 0 "

Each indented line delineates another code piece. To stroll through the above code piece, line 1 is the begin of the principle code square. Line 2 is another code area; if "x" has a quality not equivalent to 0, then indented lines underneath it will be assessed. Thus, lines 3 and 4 are in another code area and will be assessed if line 2 is valid. Line 5 is yet another code area and is just assessed if "y" is not equivalent to 0. Line 6 is a piece of the same code obstructs as lines 3 and 4; it will likewise be assessed in the same square as those lines. Line 7 is in the same segment as line 1 and is assessed paying little heed to what any indented lines may do.

You'll see that compound articulations, similar to the if examinations, are made by having the header line taken after by a colon (":"). Whatever is left of the announcement is indented underneath it. The greatest thing to re- part is that space decides gathering; if your code doesn't work for reasons unknown, twofold check which proclamations are indented.

A brisk note: the demonstration of saying "x = 1" is relegating a worth to a variable. For this situation, "x" is the variable; by definition its esteem changes. That just implies that you can give it any quality you need; for this situation the worth is "1". Variables are a standout amongst the most widely recognized programming things you will work with in light of the fact that they are what store values and are utilized as a part of information control.

5.1.2 Multiple Line Spanning

Explanations can compass more than one line in the event that they are gathered inside of supports (enclosure "()", square sections "[]", or wavy props "{}"). Regularly brackets are utilized. At the point when traversing lines inside of props, indentation doesn't make a difference; the space of the beginning section used to figure out which code area the entire articulation has a place with. String explanations can likewise be multi-line in the event that you utilize triple quotes. For instance:

Posting 5.2: Use of triple quotes

```
>>> enormous = """ This i s
... a multi-l i n e b l ock
... o f t e x t; Python puts
... an end-of-l i n e marker
... a ft e r each l i n e. """
>>>
>>> enormous
" This i s \012 a multi -l i n e piece \012 o f t e
x t; Python puts \012 an end-of -l i n e marker
\012 a ft e r each l i n e. "
```

Note that the \012 is the octal form of \n, the "newline" indicator. The ellipsis (...) above are clear lines in the intuitive Python brief used to demonstrate the mediator is sitting tight for more information.

5.2   Python Object Types

In the same way as other programming languages, Python has assembled in information sorts that the programmer uses to make his program. These information sorts are the building squares of the program. Contingent upon the language, diverse information sorts are accessible. A few languages, eminently C and C++, have extremely primitive sorts; a ton of programming time is essentially utilized around consolidate these primitive sorts into helpful information structures. Python gets rid of a considerable measure of this monotonous work. It al- prepared executes an extensive variety of sorts and structures, leaving the engineer more opportunity to really make the program. Trust me; this is one of the things I despised when I was learning C/C++. Needing to always reproduce the same information structures for each program is not something to anticipate.

Python has the accompanying inherent sorts: numbers, strings, records, lexicons, tuples, and documents. Normally, you can fabricate your own particular sorts if necessary, however Python was made so that once in a while will you need to "move your own". The inherent sorts are sufficiently intense to cover the lion's share of your code and are effortlessly upgraded. We'll complete up this segment by discussing numbers; we'll cover the others in later parts.

Before it slips my mind, I ought to specify that Python doesn't have solid coded sorts; that is, a variable can be utilized as a number, a buoy, a string, or whatever. Python will figure out what is required as it runs. See underneath:

Posting 5.3: Weak coding sorts

```
>>> x =  12

>>> y = " logger "

>>>  x 12

>>>  y

" logger "
```

Different languages frequently require the programmer to choose what the variable must be the point at which it is at first made. For instance, C would oblige you to pronounce "x" in the above program to be of sort int and "y" to be of sort string. From that point on, that is each one of those variables can be, regardless of the possibility that later on you conclude that they ought to be an alternate sort.

That implies you need to choose what every variable will be the point at which you begin your program, i.e. choosing whether a number variable ought to be a number or a skimming point number. Clearly you could backtrack and transform them at a later time yet its only one all the more thing for you to consider and recollect. Additionally, at whatever time you overlook what sort a variable is and you attempt to relegate the wrong esteem to it, you get a compiler mistake.

5.3 Python Numbers

Python can deal with typical long whole numbers (max length decided in view of the operating system, much the same as C), Python long whole numbers (max length subject to accessible memory), drifting point numbers (simply like C copies), octal and hex numbers, and complex (numbers with a fanciful part). Here are a few illustrations of these numbers:

• number: 12345, -32

• Python number: 999999999L (In Python 3.x, all whole numbers are Python whole numbers)

• skim: 1.23, 4e5, 3e-4

• octal: 012, 0456

• hex: 0xf34, 0X12FA

• complex: 3+4j, 2J, 5.0+2.5j

Python has the ordinary implicit numeric devices you'd expect: expression administrators (*, >>, +, <, and so on.), math capacities (pow, abs, and so on.), and utilities (rand, math, and so forth.). For substantial calculating Python has the Numeric Python (NumPy) augmentation that has such things as network information sorts. In the event that you require it, it must be introduced independently. It's intensely utilized as a part of science and scientific settings, as its energy and usability make it identical to Mathematica, Maple, and MatLab.

In spite of the fact that this likely doesn't mean much to non-programmers, the expression administrators found in C have been incorporated in Python, however some of them are somewhat diverse. Rationale administrators are spelled out in Python as opposed to utilizing images, e.g. intelligent AND is spoken to by "and", not by "&&"; coherent OR is spoken to by "or", not "||"; and sensible NOT utilizes "not" rather than "!". More data can be found in the Python documentation. Administrator level-of-priority is the same as C, however utilizing parentheses is exceptionally urged to guarantee the expression is assessed effectively and upgrade coherence. Blended sorts (buoy qualities joined with integer qualities) are changed over up to the most noteworthy sort before assessment, i.e. adding a buoy and a whole number will bring about the whole number to be changed to a buoy esteem before the total is as-sessed.

Catching up on what I said before, variable as-signments are created when initially utilized and don't need to be predeclared like in C.

Posting 5.4: Generic C++ illustration

```
int a = 3;/inline initialization of in
teger
```

```
float b;    //sequential initializati
on of floating point number
```

```
b = 4.0f;
```

Posting 5.5: Generic Python sample

```
>>>a = 3    #integer
```

```
>>>b = 4.0 #floating point
```

As should be obvious, "an" and "b" are both num-bers however Python can make sense of what sort they are without being told. In the C++ case, a buoy quality must be "proclaimed" twice; first the variable is given a sort ("glide") then the genuine worth is given to the variable. You'll additionally take note of that remarks in Python are situated off with a hash/pound sign (#) and are utilized precisely like the "//" remarks in C++ or Java.

That is about it for numbers in Python. It can likewise handle bit-wise control, for example, left-move and right-move, however in the event that you need to do that, then you'll presumably not have any desire to utilize Python for your undertaking. As additionally expressed, complex numbers can be utilized however in the event that you ever need to utilize them, check

CHAPTER SIX

STRINGS

Strings in programming are essentially message, either individual characters, words, expressions, or complete sentences. They are a standout amongst the most common components to utilize when programming, in any event in the matter of connecting with the client. Since they are so regular, they are a local information sort inside of Python, importance they have numerous effective abilities constructed in. Not at all like different languages, you don't need to stress over making these capacities yourself. This is great in light of the fact that the inherent ones have been tried many times over and have been optimized for execution and solidness.

Strings in Python are unique in relation to most different languages. Most importantly, there are no roast sorts, just single character strings (scorch sorts are single characters, separate from genuine strings, utilized for memory protection). Strings likewise can't be changed set up; another string article is made at whatever point you need to roll out improvements to it, for example, linking. This essentially implies you must be mindful that you are not controlling the string in memory; it doesn't get changed or erased as you work with it. You are basically making another string every time.

Here's a rundown of basic string operations:

- s1 = " : unfilled string

- s2 = "knight's" : twofold quotes

- block = """" - """" : triple-cited piece

- s1 + s2 : connect (join)

- s2 * 3 : rehash the string a specific number of times

- s2[n] : list (the position of a certain character)

- len(s2) : get the length of a string

- "a %s parrot" % "dead" : string designing (deplored in Python 3.x)

- "a {0} parrot".format("dead") : string designing (Python 3.x)

- for x in s2 : emphasis (successively travel
through the string's characters)

- 'm' in s2 : enrollment (is there a given character in the string?)

Vacant strings are composed as two quotes with
nothing in the middle. The quotes utilized can be
either single or twofold; my inclination is to utilize
twofold quotes since you don't need to escape the
single quote to utilize it in a string. That implies
you can compose an announcement like

"And after that he said, 'No chance' when I let him
know."

On the off chance that you need to utilize only one
kind of quote check constantly, you need to utilize the oblique punctuation line character to "get
away" the sought quote stamps so Python doesn't
believe its toward the end of the expression, similar to this:

"And afterward he said, \"No way\" when I let him know."

Triple cited pieces are for strings that compass various lines, as demonstrated last part. Python gathers the whole content piece into a solitary string with installed newline characters. This is useful for things like composing short passages of content, e.g. guidelines, or for designing your source code for elucidation.

6.1   Basic string operations

The "+" and "*" administrators are over-burden in Python, giving you a chance to connect and re-hash string articles, individually. Over-burdening is simply utilizing the same administrator to do numerous things, taking into account the circumstance where its utilized. For instance, the "+" image can mean expansion when two numbers are included or, as for this situation, consolidating strings.

Connecting joins two (or more) strings into another string article though rehash basically rehashes a given string a given number of times. Here are a few illustrations:

Posting 6.1: Operator over-burdening

```
>>> l e n ( " abc " ) #l e n g t h : number i tems
```

```
>>> " abc " + " def " #concatenation : a new s
t r i n g
```

" abcdef "

```
>>> " Ni ! " * 4    #m u l t i p l e concatenta-
tion : " Ni ! " + " Ni ! " + . . .
```

" Ni ! Ni ! Ni ! Ni ! "

You should be mindful that Python doesn't naturally change a number to a string, so composing "spam" + 3 will give you a blunder. To unequivocally tell Python that a number ought to be a string, just let it know. This is like throwing values in C/C++. It educates Python that the number is not a whole number or gliding point number but rather is, in all actuality, a content representation of the number. Simply recall that you can no more perform scientific capacities with it; its entirely message.

Posting 6.2: Casting a number to a string

```
>>>s t r ( 3 ) #converts number to s t r i n g
```

Cycle in strings is somewhat unique in relation to in different languages. Instead of making a circle to ceaselessly experience the string and print out every character, Python has an inherent sort for emphasis. Here's an illustration took after by a clarification:

Posting 6.3: Iteration through a string

```
>>> myjob = " logger "

>>> for c in myjob : print c , #step through i
tems

...

l u m b e r j a c k

>>> "k" in myjob   #1 implies t mourn
```

Basically what is going on is that Python is consecutively experiencing the variable "myjob" and printing every character that exists in the string. for articulations will be secured inside and out later in the book in any case, for the present simply be mindful that they are what you use to venture through a scope of qualities. As should be obvious they can be utilized for strings or, all the more regularly, numbers.

The second sample is essentially an examination. Does the letter "k" exist in the worth put away by "myjob"? On the off chance that yes, then Python will give back a numeric estimation of 1, demonstrating yes. On the off chance that "k" didn't exist, it would give back a 0. This specific case is regularly utilized as a part of word handling applications, however you can presumably consider different circumstances where it would be valuable.

6.2   Indexing and cutting strings

Strings in Python are taken care of like exhibits in C. Dissimilar to C clusters, characters inside of a string can be gotten to both front and in reverse.

Front-ways, a string begins off with a position of 0 and the character wanted is discovered through a counterbalance esteem (how far to move from the end of the string). Nonetheless, you additionally can locate this character by utilizing a negative balance esteem from the end of the string. I won't go profoundly into it, however here's a brisk illustration:

>>>S = "spam"

Posting 6.4: String indexing

>>>S [0] , S[– 2] #indexing from the f r o n t and back

(" s " , " a ")

Indexing is basically telling Python where a character can be found inside of the string. In the same way as other different languages, Python begins tallying at 0 rather than 1. So the first character's record is 0, the second character's list is 1, etc. It's the same numbering in reverse through the string, aside from that the last letter's record is -1 rather than 0 (since 0 is as of now taken). Thusly, to record the last letter you would utilize -1, the second to the last letter is -2, and so on. Knowing the list of a character is vital for cutting.

Cutting a string is essentially what it seems like: by giving upper and lower file values, we can haul out only the characters we need. An awesome case of this is when preparing an information document where every line is ended with a newline character; simply cut off the last character furthermore, prepare every line. You could likewise utilize it to process order line contentions by "sifting" out the program name. Once more, here's an illustration:

>>>S = "spam"

Posting 6.5: String cutting

```
>>>S [ 1 : 3 ] , S [ 1 : ] , S [ : – 1 ] #s l i c i n g : e
x t r a c t   s e c t i o n
```

(" dad " , 'pam " , " spa ")

You'll see that the colon image is utilized when cutting. The colon goes about as a separator between the upper and lower list values. In the event that one of those qualities is not given, Python deciphers that to imply that you need everything from the file quality to the end of the string. In the illustration over, the first cut is from file 1 (the second letter, comprehensive) to list 3 (the 4th letter, elite). You can consider the record to really be the space before every letter; that is the reason the letter "m" is excluded in the first cut yet the letter "p" is.

The second cut is from record 1 (the second letter) to the end of the string. The third cut begins toward the end of the string.

1.3   String Formatting

Formatting strings is simply a way of presenting the information on the screen in a way that conveys the information best. Some examples of formatting are creating column headers, dynamically creating a sentence from a list or stored variable, or stripping extra neousin-formation from the strings, such as excess spaces. (Python 3.x has a new way of formatting strings; this will be discussed in the section below.)

Python supports the creation of dynamic strings. What this means is that you can create a variable containing a value of some type (such as a string or number) then "call" that value into your string. You can process a string the same way as in C if you choose to, such as % d for integers and % f for floating point numbers. Here's an example:

Listing6.6: Dynamic string creation

```
>>>S="parrot"

>>>d= 1

>>>print 'Thatis %ddead%s!'
% (d, s)Thatis 1 deadparrot!
```

Pythonalsohasastring utility module-fortoolssuchascasecon-version, converting stringstonumbers,etc.Here's yetanotherex-am-ple:

Listing6.7:Stringuti-lities

```
>>>import string   #standard utilities
```

```
module
>>>S="spammify"
>>>string.upper(S) #convert to upper-
case
 'SPAMMIFY'
>>>string .find(S, "mm") #return index
of substring
3
>>>string.atoi("42"), '42' #convert
from/to string
(42, '42')
>>>string.join( string.split(S,
 "mm"), "XX")'spaXXify'
```

Notice the example of these cond to last line. Back quotes are used to convert an object into a string. This is one way around the "don't mix strings and numbers" problem from earlier. I'll leave the last line example above as a mental test. See If you can figure out what the statement is doing.

Though it's not strictly a string operation (it can be used with just about anything that can be measured), the **len()** method can be used to give you the length of a string. For example,

Listing6.8: Finding the length of a string

```
>>> string = "The Life of Brian"
>>> print len(string)17
>>> len("The Meaning of Life")19
```

As shown in these cond example above, you don't necessarily have to use a print statement (or **print ()** function in Python3.x) to display a value. Simply writing what you want will print out the result. However, this doesn't always work in your favor.

Sometimes the object will only return a memory address, as we will see later in the book. Generally speaking, it's simply easier to explicitly state "print" if you want a statement evaluated and printed out. Otherwise you don't know exactly what value it will return.

1.4   Combining and Separating Strings

Strings can be (joined) and isolated (part) effortlessly. Tokenization is the procedure of part something up into individual tokens; for this situation, a sentence is part into individual words. At the point when a page is parsed by a program, the HTML, Javascript, and whatever other code in the page is tokenized and recognized as a catchphrase, administrator, variable, and so on. The program then uses this data to show the site page effectively, or if nothing else and additionally it can.

Python does much the same thing (however with better results). The Python translator tokenizes the source code and recognizes the parts that are a piece of the genuine programming language and the parts that are information. The individual tokens are isolated by delimiters, burn acters that really isolate one token from another.

In strings, the principle delimiter is a whitespace character, for example, a tab, a newline, or a genuine space. These delimiters separate individual characters or words, sentences, and passages. At the point when unique organizing is required, different delimiters can be indicated by the programmer.

Joining strings joins the different strings into one string. Be- reason string operations dependably make another string, you don't need to stress over the first strings being overwritten. The catch is that it doesn't link the strings, i.e. joining doesn't consolidate them like you would anticipate. Here's an illustration:

Posting 6.9: Joining strings

```
>>>string1 = " 1 2 3 "
>>>string2= "A B C"
>>>string3 = string2.join(string1)
```

```
>>>print s t r i n g 3
```

1A B C A B C2A B C A B C3

As should be obvious, the outcomes are not what you anticipate. In any case, when making a perplexing string, it can be ideal to put the pieces into a rundown and after that basically go along with them, as opposed to attempting to connect them.

Said quickly some time recently, I will talk somewhat more about concate- country. Connecting consolidates two or more strings into another, complete string. This is likely what you were thinking when I discussed joining strings together.

Posting 6.10: String linking

```
>>>s t r i n g 1 + s t r i n g 2 " 1  2  3A B C "
```

```
>>>"Navy sauce . " + "The f i n e s t sauce in
the Navy . " Navy sauce . The f i n e s t sauce in
the Navy .
```

Odds are you will utilize linking more regularly than joining. To me, it basically bodes well than upsetting join(). Yet, with practice, you may discover joining to be simpler or more productive.

At last, part strings isolates them into their segment parts. The outcome is a rundown containing the individual words or characters. Here are a few illustrations:

Posting 6.11: Splitting strings

```
>>>s t r i n g = "My w i f e loathes spam . "
>>>s t r i n g . s p l i t ( ) # s p l i t s t r i n g at spaces
[ 'My " , " w i f e " , " loathes " , " spam . " ]
>>>n ew_ string = " 1 , 2 , 3 "
>>>n ew_ string . s p l i t ( " , " ) # s p l i t s t r i n g at commas
[ " 1 " , " 2 " , " 3 " ]
```

Note how the new_string was part precisely at the commas; the main spaces before the numbers was incorporated in the yield. You ought to be mindful of how your yield will be when characterizing the separating characters.

As we move further into the Python language, we will take a gander at these and different components of strings. Support programs will advantage most from figuring out how to utilize strings, on the other hand, word processors are clearly somewhere else where knowing how to control strings will prove to be useful.

One last note: including a comma toward the end of a print line keeps Python from naturally making a newline. This is most viable when making tables and you don't need everything in a solitary segment. A helpful reference of the most widely recognized string systems can be found on page 154 in the index. These routines perform musical show tions, for example, part() indicated above, decreasing the measure of work you need to do physically and giving a bigger toolset to you to utilize.

6.5   Regular Expressions

I'm not going to dig into customary expressions in this book. They are on the verge of excessively confused for an initial book. Notwithstanding,

I will quickly disclose so individuals new to programming see how capable of an apparatus normal expressions are.

General expressions (regex) are institutionalized expressions that permit you to pursuit, supplant, and parse content. Basically, it's similar to utilizing the discover/supplant instrument in a word processor. Then again, regex is a mind boggling, formal language design that permits you to do a considerable measure more with strings than the typical strategies permit you to do. In all honesty, however, I have never utilized consistent expressions, essentially in light of the fact that my programs so far haven't obliged it.

Really, in the event that you can get by with the typical string routines, then by all methods use them. They are speedy, simple, and make it straightforward your code. Notwithstanding, regex explanations can bode well than long, complex if/else conditions or daisy-affixed string techniques.

On the off chance that you feel the need to utilize standard expressions, please counsel the Python documentation discussing customary expressions. There is a considerable measure of data there and regex is on the verge of excessively progressed for this book; there are books singularly committed to regex and I don't think I can do the theme equity.

CHAPTER SEVEN

LISTS

Records in Python are a standout amongst the most flexible accumulation article sorts accessible. The other two sorts are lexicons and tuples, yet they are truly more like varieties of records.

Python records take the necessary steps of the vast majority of the gathering information structures found in different languages and since they are constructed in, you don't need to stress over physically making them. Records can be utilized for any sort of item, from numbers and strings to more records. They are gotten to simply like strings (e.g. cutting and linking) so they are easy to utilize and they're variable length, i.e. they develop and shrivel consequently as they're utilized. In all actuality, Python records are C clusters inside the Python translator and act simply like a variety of pointers.

So hopefully you comprehend what precisely I'm looking at, Listing 7.1 demonstrates several snappy illustrations that makes a rundown and afterward does two or three controls to it.

Posting 7.1: Generic rundown illustrations

```
>>>list = [1, 2, 3, 4, 5]

>>>print list

[1, 2, 3, 4, 5]

>>>print list[0] #print the list thing at
record 0

1

>>>list.pop() #remove and print the la
st thing

5

>>>print list #show t cap the last thing
was uprooted

[1, 2, 3, 4]
```

Here's a rundown of normal rundown operations:

- L1 = [] A vacant rundown

- L2 = [0, 1, 2, 3] Four things

- L3 = ['abc', ['def', 'ghi']] Nested sublists

- L2 [n], L3[n][j] L2[n:j], len(L2) Index, cut, length

- L1 + L2, L2 * 3 Concatenate, rehash

- for x in L2, 3 in L2 Iteration, enrollment

- L2.append(4), L2.sort(), L2.index(1), L2.reverse() Methods: develop, sort, pursuit, reverse, and so on.

- del L2[k], L2[n:j] = [] Shrinking

- L2[n] = 1, L2[n:j] = [4,5,6] Index task, cut task

- range(4), xrange(0, 4) Make records/tuples of whole numbers

The greatest thing to recall is that rundowns are a progression of articles composed inside square sections, isolated by commas. Lexicons and tuples will appear to be comparative aside from they have diverse sorts of sections.

7.1   List utilization

Records are frequently used to store homogeneous qualities, i.e. a rundown typically holds names, numbers, or different successions that are every one of the one information sort. They don't need to; they can be utilized with whatever information sorts you need to blend and match. It's fair ordinarily less demanding to think about a rundown as holding a "standard" grouping of things.

The most well-known utilization of a rundown is to emphasize over the rundown and perform the same activity to every article inside of the rundown, subsequently the utilization of comparable information sorts. Time for a sample:

Posting 7.2: Iterating through a rundown

```
>>> mylist = [ "one" , "two", "thre" ]
>>> for x in mylist:
...    print " number " + x
...
```

number one number two number t h r e

In the above illustration, a rundown of content strings was made. Next, a straightforward for circle was utilized to emphasize through the rundown, prepending "number" to every rundown protest and printing them out. We will discuss for circles later however this is a typical utilization of them.

One thing to note at this moment, on the other hand, is that you can utilize whatever worth for "x" that you need, i.e. you can utilize whatever name you need rather than "x". I say this in light of the fact that it sort of stunned me when I initially experienced it in Python. In different languages, circles like this are either hard-wired into the language and you need to utilize its organization or you need to explicitly make the "x" esteem heretofore so you can call it on the up and up. Python's way is much simpler in light of the fact that you can utilize whatever name bodes well, or you can basically utilize a "non specific variable" as I did. Case in point, I could have utilized "for num in mylist:" or some other variety to repeat through the rundown. It's all up to you.

I won't go into the straightforward activities for records since they work simply like string operations. You can list, cut, and control the rundown like you can for strings. As a general rule, a string is more like an altered rundown that just handles alphanumeric characters.

On the off chance that you have inquiries, take a gander at the part on Strings (Chapter 6); on the off chance that regardless you have inquiries, take a gander at the official Python documentation. Simply recall that the subsequent article will be another rundown (encompassed by square sections) and not a string, numbers, and so on.

7.2 Adding List Elements

Adding new things to a rundown is greatly simple. You essentially advise the rundown to include it. Same thing with sorting a rundown

Posting 7.3: Adding things to a rundown

```
>>>n e w l i s t = [ 1 , 2 , 3 ]
>>>n e w l i s t . attach ( 5 4 )
>>>n e w l i s t
[ 1 , 2 , 3 , 5 4 ]
>>>a _ l i s t = [ " eat " , "ham" , "Spam" , "
eggs " , " and" ]
>>>a _ l i s t . s o r t ( ) #s o r t l i s t i tems ( c a
p i t a l l e t e r s come f i r s t )
>>>a _ l i s t
```

[" Spam " , " and " , " eat " , " eggs " , 'ham "]

The attach() system basically adds a solitary thing to the end of a rundown; it's unique in relation to connecting since it takes a solitary article and not a rundown. affix() and sort() both change the rundown set up and don't make a just took the ribbon off new rundown object, nor do they give back the altered rundown. To view the progressions, you need to explicitly call the rundown protest once more, as indicated in Listing 7.3. So be informed regarding that in the event that you are confounded about whether the progressions really occurred.

On the off chance that you need to put the new thing in a particular position in the rundown, you need to tell the rundown which position it ought to be in, i.e. you need to utilize the list of what the position is. Keep in mind, the record begins at 0, not 1, as demonstrated in Listing 7.4.

Posting 7.4: Adding things by means of indexing

```
>>>newlist.insert(1, 69)        #inser
t " 69 " at  record " 1 "
```

```
>>>newlist
[1, 69, 2, 3, 54]
```

You can add a second rundown to a current one by utilizing the broaden() technique. Basically, the two rundowns are (connected) together, similar to so:

Posting 7.5: Combining records

```
>>>newerlist = [ "Mary", " had, " a", "li
tle", "spam
```

```
."]
>>>newlist.expand(newerlist) #ex-
```
tending with named list

```
>>> newlist
```

[1, 69, 2, 3, 54, "Mary", "had", "a", "l
itle", "spam."]

```
>>>newerlist.expand(["It"s", "gre
ase", "was", "white", "as", "snow."])
```
#extending inline

```
>>> newerlist
```

["Mary", "had", "a", "litle", "spam.",
"It"s", "grease", "was", "white", "as
", "snow."]

Be mindful, there is a particular contrast in the
middle of broaden and affix. expand() takes a solitary contention, which is dependably a rundown,
and includes each of the components of that rundown to the first rundown; the two rundowns are
converged into one. add() takes one contention,

which can be any information sort, and basically adds it to the end of the rundown; you wind up with a rundown that has one component which is the attached article. Here's an illustration from "Plunge into Python":

Posting 7.6: Extend versus affix

```
>>> li = [ " a ", " b ", " c " ]
>>> li . augment ( [ " d ", " e ", " f " ] )

>>> li
[ " a ", " b ", " c ", " d ", " e ", " f " ]
#merged list
>>> len(li)        #list length
>>> li [ - 1 ]        #reverse  record
" f "
>>> li = [ " a ", " b ", " c " ]
>>> li . affix ( [ " d ", " e ", " f " ] )        #list
```

o b j e c t utilized as an component

```
>>> li
[ " a ", " b ", " c ", [ " d ", " e ", " f " ]
>>> l e n ( l i ) 4
>>> li [ - 1 ]        #the s i n g l e l i s t o b j e c
t
['d', 'e', 'f']
```

7.3   Mutability

An exceptional aspect concerning records is that they are variable, i.e. they can be changed set up without making another article. The enormous concern with this is recalling that, on the off chance that you do this, it can influence different references to it. Notwithstanding, this isn't generally a vast issue so it's a greater amount of something to remember on the off chance that you get program blunders.

Here's an illustration of changing a rundown utilizing counterbalance and cutting:

Posting 7.7: Changing a rundown

```
>>> L = [ " spam " , " Spam " , 'SPAM! " ]

>>> L [ 1 ] = " eggs " #index task

>>> L
```

[" spam " , " eggs " , 'SPAM! "]

```
>>> L [ 0 : 2 ] = [ " eat " , " more " ] #s l i c e
task : d e l e t e+i n s e r t

>>> L #r e p l a c e s i tems listed at 0 and 1
```

[" eat " , " more " , 'SPAM! "]

Since records are changeable, you can likewise utilize the del proclamation to erase a thing or area. Here's a case:

```
>>> L
```

Posting 7.8: Deleting rundown things

['SPAM! " , " eat " , " more " , " p l e a s e "]

```
>>> del L [ 0 ] #d e l e t e one thing

>>> L
```

[" eat " , " more " , " p l e a s e "]

>>> del L [1 :] #d e l e t e an e n t i r e s e c t
i o n

>>> L #same as L [1 :] = [ ]

[" eat "]

7.4 Methods

I've said systems already and I'll discuss routines
all the more in the item situated programming
section, however for the inquisitive, a system
works like a capacity, in that you have the strategy
name taken after by contentions in brackets. The
enormous distinction is that a system is qualified
to a particular item with the period accentuation
mark. In a portion of the cases over, the rundown
article was influenced by a strategy utilizing the
"." (dab) terminology. The "." advised the Python
mediator to search for the system name that took
after the spot and perform the activities in the
technique on the related rundown object.

Since everything in Python is an article, about everything has an a technique. You presumably won't have the capacity to recollect all the techniques for each and every article sort, yet recalling the most widely recognized and helpful ones will accelerate advancement. Having a rundown of the routines for every item sort is exceptionally helpful. You'll discover arrangements of the most widely recognized routines for every item sort in the reference sections of this book.

At last, you have to recall that just variable articles can be changed set up; strings, tuples, and different items will dependably need to make new questions in the event that you transform them. You additionally need to recall that adjusting an article set up can influence different articles that allude to it.

A complete posting of rundown routines can be found on page 160 in the supplement.

CHAPTER EIGHT

DICTIONARIES

By records, word references are a standout amongst the most valuable information sorts in Python. Python word references are unordered accumulations of items, coordinated to a catchphrase. Python records, then again, are requested accumulations that utilization a numerical balance.

As a result of their development, word references can supplant numerous "typical" pursuit calculations and information structures found in C and related languages. For those originating from different languages, Python dictionaries are much the same as a hash table, where an item is mapped to a key name.

Lexicons incorporate the accompanying properties:

1. Accessed by watchword, not a balance. Word references are like cooperative clusters. Everything in the word reference has a relating catchphrase; the watchword is utilized to "call" the thing.

2. Stored items are in an arbitrary request to give quicker lookup. At the point when made, a word reference stores things in any request it picks. To get a worth, basically supply the key. On the off chance that you have to request the things inside of a word reference, you need to do it without anyone else's help; there are no implicit routines for it.

3. Dictionaries are variable length, can hold objects of any sort (counting different word references), and bolster profound settling (multiple levels of things can be in a lexicon, for example, a rundown inside of a word reference inside another lexicon).

4. They are changeable however can't be adjusted like records or strings; they are the main information sort that backings mapping.

5. Internally, lexicons are actualized as a hash table. Here's the (now standard) rundown of regular operations:

- d1 = {} Empty lexicon

- d2 = {'spam' : 2, "eggs" : 3} Two-thing lexicon

- d3 = {'food' : {'ham' : 1, "egg" : 2}} Nesting

- d2['eggs'], d3['food']['ham'] Indexing by key

- d2.has_key('eggs'), d2.keys(), d2.values() Methods: part boat test, keys rundown, qualities list, and so on.

- len(d1) Length (number put away passages)

- d2[key] = new, del d2[key] Adding/changing, erasing

8.1   Making a word reference

As beforehand expressed, you make lexicons and access things through a key. The key can be of any changeless sort, similar to a string, number, or tuple. The qualities can be any sort of item, including different word references. The arrangement for making a lexicon is indicated in Listing 8.1:

Posting 8.1: Dictionary design

```
>>>d i c t i o n a r y = {" key  name" : " esteem }
```

Be that as it may, the key name and quality can be anything permitted, such as:

Posting 8.2: Dictionary keys illustration

```
>>>d i c t i o n a r y = {"cow" : " horse shelter " ,
1 : " pig " ,  2 : [ "spam" , " green " ,  " corn " ] }
```

Notice that the sections for word references are wavy props, the separator between a catchphrase and it's related worth is a colon, and that every key/quality is isolated by a comma. This are only a percentage of the things that can bring about language structure lapses in your program.

8.2   Basic operations

The len() capacity can be utilized to give the quantity of things put away in a lexicon or the length of the key rundown. The keys() strategy gives back all the keys in the lexicon as a rundown. Here's a couple of cases:

Posting 8.3: Some lexicon routines

```
>>> d2 = { " spam " : 2 , 'ham " : 1 , " eggs " : 3 }
>>> d2 [ " spam " ] #fetch esteem for key
2
>>> len ( d2 ) #number of entries in dictionary
3
>>> d2 . has_key ( 'ham " )        #does the key exist ? ( 1 methods t lament )
1
>>> d2 . keys ( )    #list of keys
[ " eggs " , " spam " , 'ham " ]
```

Since word references are impermanent, you can add and erase qualities to them without making another lexicon object. Simply relegate a quality to a key to change or make a section and utilization del to erase an item connected with a given key.

Posting 8.4: Modifying lexicons

>>> d2 ['ham "] = [" g r i l " , " prepare " , " f r y "]   # change section

>>> d2

{ " eggs " : 3 , " spam " : 2 , 'ham " : [" g r i l " , " prepare " , " f r y "] }

>>> del d2 [" eggs "]   #d e l e t e section construct with respect to pivotal word

>>> d2

{ " spam " : 2 , 'ham " : [" g r i l " , " prepare " , " f r y "] }

>>> d2 [" early lunch "] = " Bacon '   #add new section

>>> d2

{ " early lunch " : " Bacon " , 'ham " : [" g r i l " , " prepare " , " f r y "

] , " spam " : 2}

To contrast and records, adding another item to

a lexicon just obliges making another magic word and quality. Records will give back a "record too far out" blunder if the counterbalance is past the end of the rundown. Along these lines you must affix or cut to add qualities to records.

Here is a more sensible word reference case. The accompanying illustration makes a table that maps programming language names (the keys) to their inventors (the qualities). You get an inventor name by indexing on language name:

Posting 8.5: Using a word reference

```
>>> t a b l e = { " Python " : " Guido van Ros-
sum " ,
...     ' Perl " : " Larry  Wall " ,
...     ' Tcl " : " John Ousterhout " }
...
>>> language = " Python "
>>> c r e a t o r = t a b l e [ language ]
>>> c r e a t o r
```

" Guido van Rossum "

```
>>> for lang in table.keys(): print
lang, '\t", table[lang]
```

```
...
```

Tcl John Ousterhout Python Guido van Rossum Perl Larry Wall

From this case, you may see that the last summon
is like string and rundown emphasis utilizing the
for order. Then again, you'll likewise see that, since
word references aren't successions, you can't utilize the standard for explanation. You must utilize
the keys() technique to give back a rundown of all
the essential words which you can then emphasize
through like an ordinary rundown.

You may have additionally seen that word references can act like light- weight databases. The
sample above makes a table, where the genius
gramming language "section" is coordinated by
the maker's "column". On the off chance that you
have a requirement for a database, you may need
to think about utilizing as a lexicon. On the off

chance that the information will fit, you will spare yourself a considerable measure of superfluous coding and lessen the cerebral pains you would get from managing an all out database. Truly, you don't have the flexibility and force of a genuine database, however for no-nonsense arrangements, lexicons

8.3   Dictionary subtle elements

1. Sequence operations don't work. As beforehand expressed, dictionaries are mappings, not successions. Since there's no request to word reference things, capacities like linking and cutting don't work.

2. Assigning new files includes sections. Keys can be made when making a lexicon (i.e. when you at first make the dictionary) or by adding new values to a current word reference. The procedure is comparable and the final result is the same.

3. Keys can be anything unchanging. The past samples indicated keys as string items, how-

ever any non-alterable item (like records)
can be utilized for a decisive word. Numbers
can be utilized to make a rundown like article however without the requesting. Tuples
(secured later) are once in a while used to
make compound keys; class occurrences (likewise secured later) that are composed not to
change can likewise be utilized if necessary.

All things considered, we're almost finished with
Python sorts. The following section will cover tuples, which are essentially permanent records.

8.4 Operation

Like alternate parts, a rundown of regular word
reference operations can be found in the index on
page 162.

CHAPTER NINE

TUPLES

The last inherent information sort is the tuple. Python tuples work exactly like Python records with the exception of they are permanent, i.e. they can't be changed set up. They are ordinarily composed inside enclosures to recognize them from records (which utilize square sections), however as you'll see, brackets aren't generally vital. Since tuples are changeless, their length is settled. To develop or therapist a tuple, another tuple must be made.

Here's a rundown of regular operations for tuples:

- () A vacant tuple

- t1 = (0,) An one-thing tuple (not an expression)

- t2 = (0, 1, 2, 3) A four-thing tuple

- t3 = 0, 1, 2, 3 Another four-thing tuple (same as former line, simply less the bracket)

- t3 = ('abc', ('def', 'ghi')) Nested tuples

- t1[n], t3[n][j] Index

- t1[i:j], Slice

- len(tl) Length

- t1 + t2 Concatenate

- t2 * 3 Repeat

- for x in t2, Iteration

- 3 in t2 Membership

The second section demonstrates to make an one thing tuple. Since paren- postulations can encompass expressions, you need to show Python when a solitary thing is really a tuple by putting a comma after the thing. The fourth passage demonstrates a tuple without enclosures; this structure can be utilized when a tuple is unambiguous. On the other hand, it's least demanding to simply utilize brackets than to make sense of when they're discretionary.

9.1 Why Use Tuples?

Tuples regularly store heterogeneous information, like how records typically hold homogeneous information. It's not a hard-coded control but rather basically a tradition that some Python programmers take after. Since tuples are unchanging, they can be utilized to store diverse information around a certain thing. Case in point, a contact rundown could possibly put away inside of a tuple; you could have a name and location (both strings) in addition to a telephone number (whole number) inside on information object.

The greatest thing to recollect is that standard operations like cutting and emphasis return new tuple objects. In my programming, I like utilization records for everything with the exception of when I don't need an accumulation to change. It eliminates the quantity of accumulations to consider, in addition to tuples don't give you a chance to add new things to them or erase information. You need to make another tuple in those cases.

There are a couple times when you essentially

need to utilize a tuple in light of the fact that your code obliges it. Nonetheless, a great deal of times you never know precisely what you're going to do with your code and having the adaptability of records can be helpful.

So why use tuples? Aside from now and again being the best way to make your code work, there are couples of different motivations to utilize tuples:

- Tuples are prepared speedier than records. In the event that you are making a constant arrangement of qualities that won't change, and you have to just repeat through them, utilize a tuple.

- The groupings inside of a tuple are basically shielded from modification. Thusly, you won't coincidentally change the qualities, nor would someone be able to abuse an API to adjust the information. (An API is an application programming interface. It permits programmers to utilize a program without needing to know the points of interest of the entire program.)

- Tuples can be utilized as keys for lexicons. Genuinely, I don't think I've ever utilized this, nor would I be able to think about a period when you would need to. However, there on the off chance that you ever need to utilize it

- Tuples are utilized as a part of string organizing, by holding various qualities to be embedded into a string. On the off chance that you don't recollect, here's a snappy case:

Posting 9.1: String designing with tuples

```
>>>val 1 = " i n t e g e r "

>>>val 2 = 2

>>>"The %s esteem i s rise to to %d" % ( val 1 , val 2 ) " The i n t e g e r e value i s equal to 2 '
```

9.2   Sequence Unpacking

In this way, to make a tuple, we treat it like a run-down (simply recalling to change the sections).

Posting 9.2: Packing a tuple

```
>>>tuple = (1, 2, 3, 4)
```

The expression for this is pressing a tuple, in light of the fact that the information is "stuffed into" the tuple, all wrapped up and prepared to go. Thus, to expel things from a tuple you just unload it.

Posting 9.3: Unpacking a tuple

```
>>> first, second, third, fourth = tuple
>>> first1
>>> second
2
>>> third3
>>> fourth4
```

Flawless, huh? One advantage of tuple pressing/unloading is that you can swap things set up. With different languages, you need to make the rationale to swap variables; with tuples, the rationale is natural in the information sort.

Posting 9.4: set up variable swapping

>>> bug = " w e v i l "

>>> feathered creature = " African swallow "

>>> bug , feathered creature = winged animal , bug

>>> bug

" African swallow "

>>> fledgling " w e v i l "

Tuple unloading and set up swapping are one of the neatest features of Python, as I would see it. As opposed to making the rationale to draw everything from an accumulation and spot it in its own particular variable, tuple un- pressing permits you to do everything in one stage. Set up swapping is additionally an alternate way; you don't have to make transitory variables to hold the qualities as you switch places.

9.3   Methods

Tuples have no strategies. Too bad.

All the better you can do with tuples is cutting,

emphasis, pressing and unloading. Nonetheless, Python has a perfect little trap on the off chance that you require more adaptability with tuples: you can transform them into records. Basically utilize the rundown() capacity approach a tuple and it mystically turns into a rundown. Oppositely, you can call tuple() on a rundown and it turns into a tuple.

Posting 9.5: Converting records and tuples

```
>>> my_ l ist = [ " moose", " Sweden", " l lama
" ]

>>> my_tuple = ( " Norwegian Blue ", " p ar r
ot ", " pet shop " )

>>> t u p l e ( my_ l ist )

( " moose ", " Sweden ", " l lama " )

>>> l i s t ( my_tuple )

[ " Norwegian Blue ", " p ar ro t ", " pet shop "
]
```

Clearly the advantage to this is that you can discretionarily switch between the two, contingents upon what you have to do. In the event that, part of the way through your program, you understand that you should have the capacity to control a tuple yet you don't need it to be constantly modifiable, you can make another variable that calls the rundown() work on the tuple and afterward utilize the new rundown as required.

Thus, now that we have the basic building pieces down, we can proceed onward to how you utilize them practically speaking. Then again, we'll cover one final fundamental device that everything programmers need to know how to utilize: documents.

CHAPTER TEN

FILES

The last implicit item kind of Python permits us to get to documents. The open() capacity makes a Python document object, which connections to an outside record. After a record is opened, you can read and keep in touch with it like ordinary.

Records in Python are not the same as the past sorts I've covered. They aren't numbers, arrangements, or mappings; they just fare strategies for regular document preparing. Actually, documents are a prebuilt C expansion that gives a wrapper to the C studio (standard in- put/yield) file system. In the event that you know how to utilize C documents, you essentially know how to utilize Python records.

Documents are an approach to spare information for all time. All that you've adapted so far is inhabitant just in memory; when you close down

Python or kill your PC, it goes away. You would need to retype everything over on the off chance that you needed to utilize it once more.

The records that Python makes are controlled by the PC's record system. Python has the capacity utilization operating system particular capacities to import, spare, and alter records. It might be a tad bit of work to make certain elements work accurately in cross-stage way however it implies that your program will have the capacity to be utilized by more individuals. Obviously, in the event that you are composing your program for a particular operating system, then you just need to stress over the OS-particular capacities.

10.1 File Operations

To keep things predictable, here's the rundown of Python document operations:

- output = open('/tmp/spam', 'w') Create yield record ('w' means compose)

- input = open('data', 'r') Create info document ('r' means read)

- S = input.read() Read whole document into a solitary string

- S = input.read(N) Read N number of bytes (1 or more)

- S = input.readline() Read next line (through end-line marker)

- L = input.readlines() Read whole record into rundown of line strings

- output.write(S) Write string S onto record

- output.writelines(L) Write all line strings in rundown L onto record

- output.close() Manual close (or its defeated you when automat- ically gathered)

Since Python has an inherent trash specialist, you don't generally need to physically close your records; once an item is no more referenced inside of memory, the object's memory space is consequently recovered. This applies to all articles in Python, including documents. On the other hand, its prescribed to physically close documents in vast systems; it won't hurt anything and it's great to get into the propensity in the event that you ever need to work in a language that doesn't have trash accumulation.

10.2 Files and Streams

Originating from a Unix-foundation, Python regards records as an information stream, i.e. every record is read and put away as a consecutive stream of bytes. Every document has an end-of-record (EOF) marker signifying when the last byte of information has been read from it. This is valuable on the grounds that you can compose a program that peruses a record in pieces instead of stacking the whole document into memory at one time. At the point when the end-of-document marker is come to, your

program knows there is nothing further to peruse and can proceed with whatever handling it needs to do.

At the point when a document is read, for example, with a readline() strategy, the end of the record is demonstrated at the summon line with an unfilled string; vacant lines are just strings with an end-of-line character. Here's a sample:

Posting 10.1: End of File illustration

```
>>> myfile = open ("myfile", 'w")
#open/create file for information

>>> myfile.write("helo text file")
#write a line of text

>>> myfile.close()

>>> myfile = open ("myfile", "r")
#open for yield

>>> myfile.readline() #read the line
back

"helo text file"

>>> myfile.readline()

" " #empty string indicates end of file
```

10.3 Creating a File

Making a document is amazingly simple with Python. As demonstrated in the case above, you essentially make the variable that will speak to the record, open the document, give it a filename, and advise Python that you need to keep in touch with it.

On the off chance that you don't explicitly advise Python that you need to keep in touch with a record, it will be opened in read-just mode. This goes about as a security highlight to keep you from unintentionally overwriting documents. Notwithstanding the standard "w" to show composing and "r" for perusing, Python bolsters a few other record access modes.

- "a": Appends all yield to the end of the record; does not overwrite data presently show. On the off chance that the showed document does not exist, it is made.

- "r": Opens a record for data (perusing). On the off chance that the document does not exist, an IOError exemption is raised. (Exemptions are secured in Chapter 14.)

- "r+": Opens a document for info and yield. On the off chance that the record does not exist, causes an IOError exemption.

- "w": Opens a document for yield (composing). On the off chance that the record exists, it is overwritten. On the off chance that the record does not exist, one is made.

- "w+": Opens a document for info and yield. On the off chance that the record exists, it is overwritten; generally one is made.

- "ab", "rb", "r+b", "wb", "w+b": Opens a document for twofold (i.e., non-content) info or yield. [Note: These modes are bolstered just on the Windows and Macintosh stages. Unix-like sys- tems couldn't care less about the information type.]

At the point when utilizing standard records, the vast majority of the data will be alphanumeric in nature, thus the additional twofold mode document operations. Unless you have a particular need, this will be fine for the vast majority of your assignments. In a later area, I will discuss sparing records that are included records, lexicons, or

10.4   Reading From a File

On the off chance that you see in the above run-down, the standard read-modes deliver an I/O (data/yield) blunder if the record doesn't exist. In the event that you wind up with this blunder, your program will end and give you a slip message, as underneath:

Posting 10.2: Input/Output blunder illustration

>>> f i l e = open (" m y f i l e " , " r ") Trace-back (most r e c e n t c a l l a s t) : F i l e "<st-din >", l i n e 1 , in <module>

IOError : [Errno 2] No such f i l e or d i r e c t o r y : " m y f i l e "

>>>

To settle this, you ought to constantly open documents so as to catch the lapse before it murders your program. This is called "getting the exemption", on the grounds that the IOError given is really a special case given by the Python mediator. There is a part devoted to special case taking care of (Chapter 14) however here is a brief review.

When you are performing an operation where there is a potential for a special case to happen, you ought to wrap that operation inside of an attempt/aside from code piece. This will attempt to run the operation; if an exception is tossed, you can get it and manage it smoothly. Something else, your program bites it hard.

All in all, how would you handle potential special case slips? Simply give it an attempt. (Apologies, awful joke)

Posting 10.3: Catching slips, section 1

1. >>> f = open (" m y f i l e " , "w")

2. >>> f . w r i t e (" h e l o there , my t e xt f i l e . \ n Will you f an i l g r a c e f u l y ?")

3. >>> f . c l o s e ( )

4. >>> attempt :

5. ...f i l e = open (" m y f i l e " , " r ")

6. ...f i l e . r e a d l i n e s ( )

7. ...f i l e . c l o s e ( )

8. . . . except IOError :

9. . . . print "The f i l e doesn " t e x i s t "

10. . . .

11. [" h e l o there , my t e x t f i l e . \ n " , "
    Will you f a n i l g r a c e f u l y ? "]

12. >>>

What's going ahead here? All things considered, the initial few lines are basically the same as first case in this part, then we set up an attempt/aside from piece to effortlessly open the document. The accompanying steps apply to Listing 10.3.

1. We open the document to permit keeping in touch with it.

2. The information is composed to the document.

3. The document is shut.

4. The attempt piece is made; the lines beneath that are indented are a piece of this square. Any blunders in this square are gotten by the

aside from articulation.

5. The record is opened for perusing.

6. The entire record is read and yield. (The read-lines() system gives back a rundown of the lines in the document, isolated at the newline character.)

7. The record is shut once more.

8. If an exemption was raised when the record is opened, the with the exception of line ought to catch it and procedure whatever is inside of the special case square. For this situation, it essentially prints out that the document doesn't exist.

Things being what they are, what happens if the special case does happen? This:

>>> attempt :

Posting 10.4: Catching blunders, section 2

```
...     file3 = open ( " file3 ", " r " )
...     file3.readlines ( )
```

```
...    file3.close()

...    except IOError :

...            print "The file doesn"t exist.
Check filename."

...

The file doesn"t exist.Check filename
.

>>>
```

The document "file3" hasn't been made, so obviously there is nothing to open. Typically you would get an IOError yet since you are explicitly searching for this mistake, you can deal with it. At the point when the special case is raised, the program smoothly exits and prints out the data you instructed it to.

One last note: when utilizing records, it's essential to close them when you're set utilizing them. Despite the fact that Python has constructed in waste collection, and it will generally close documents when they are no more utilized, periodically the

PC "loses track" of the records and doesn't close them when they are no more required. Open records devour system assets and, contingent upon the document mode, different programs will be unable to get to open documents.

10.5 Iterating Through Files

I've discussed emphasis before and we'll discuss it in later chapters. Cycle is basically performing an operation on information in a sequential design, typically through the for circle. With records, cycle can be utilized to peruse the data in the document and procedure it in an organized way. It additionally restrains the measure of memory taken up when a record is read, which decreases system asset use as well as enhance execution.

Let's assume you have a document of plain data, e.g. a finance document. You need to peruse the record and print out every line, with "really" arranging so it is anything but difficult to peruse. Here's a sample of how to do that. (We're assuming that the data has as of now been put in the document. Additionally, the ordinary Python translator prompts aren't noticeable in light of the fact that you would really compose this as an all out program, as we'll see later. At last, the print explanations are not perfect with Python 3.x.) attempt :

Posting 10.5: Inputting even information

```
file = open ( " p a y r o l " , " r " )
```

but IOError :

```
print "The file doesn " t e x i s t . Check file
n a m e . "
```

```
i n d i v i d u a l s = file . r e a d l i n e s ( )
```

```
print " Account " . l j u s t ( 10 ),   #comma counteracts newline
```

```
print "Name" . l j u s t ( 10 ),
```

```
print "Sum" . r j u s t ( 10 )
```

```
for r ec or d in i n d i v i d u a l s : sections = re
co r d . s p l i t ( ) print sections [ 0 ] . l j u s t ( 10
) print sections [ 1 ] . l j u s t ( 10 ) print sections
[ 2 ] . r j u s t ( 10 )
```

```
file.close()
```

Here is the means by which the yield ought to be shown on the screen (or on paper if sent to a printer).

Account	Name	Balance
101	Jeffrey	100.50
105	Patrick	325.49
110	Susan	210.50

An alternate way would be revising the four piece so it doesn't need to repeat through the variable people yet to just read the record specifically, accordingly:

```
for record in file:
```

This will emphasize through the document, read every line, and appoint it to "record". This outcomes in every line being handled quickly, instead of needing to sit tight for the whole record to be read into memory. The readlines() system obliges the record to be put in memory before it can be prepared; for substantial records, this can bring about an execution hit.

10.6 Seeking

Looking for is the procedure of moving a pointer inside of a record to a self-assertive position. This permits you to go anyplace inside of the document without needing to begin toward the starting assuredly.

The look for() strategy can take a few contentions. The primary argument (counterbalance) is beginning position of the pointer. The second, discretionary contention is the look for course from where the balance begins. 0 is the default esteem and demonstrates a balance in respect to the start of the document, 1 is in respect to the present position inside of the record, and 2 is with respect to the end of the record.

Posting 10.6: File looking for

f i l e . look for (1 5) #move pointer 15 bytes from starting o f f i l e

f i l e . look for (12 , 1) #move pointer 12 bytes from current l o c a t i o n f i l e . look for (−50 , 2) #move pointer 50 bytes in reverse from end o f f i l e

f i l e . look for (0 , 2) #move pointer at end o f f i l e

The tell() system gives back the present position of the pointer inside of the record. This can be helpful for investigating (to verify the pointer is really in the area you think it is) or as a returned quality for a capacity.

10.7 Serialization

Serialization (pickling) permits you to spare non-literary data to memory or transmit it more than a system. Pickling basically takes any information article, for example, lexicons, records, or even class examples (which we'll cover later), and proselytes it into a byte set that can be utilized to "reconstitute" the first information.

Posting 10.7: Pickling information

>>>import c P i c k l e #import c Pickle l i b r a r y

```
>>>a_list = [ " one " , " two", " clasp ",
"my" , " shoe " ]

>>>save_file = open ( " p i c k l e d _ l i s t "
, "w" )

>>>cPickle.dump( a_list, save_file)
#serializelist to file

>>> file.close()

>>>open_file = open ( " p i c k l e d _ l i s t "
, " r " )

>>>b_list = cPickle.load ( open_file
)
```

There are two distinctive pickle libraries for Python: cPickle and pickle. In the above sample, I utilized the cPickle library as opposed to the pickle library. The reason is identified with the data examined in Chapter 2. Since Python is deciphered, it runs somewhat slower contrasted with aggregated languages, similar to C. In view of this, Python has a precompiled variant of pickle that was composed in C; consequently cPickle. Utilizing cPickle makes your program run speedier.

Obviously, with processor velocities getting quicker constantly, you likely won't see a noteworthy distinction. Be that as it may, it is there and the utilization is the same as the typical pickle library, so you should use it. (As an aside, at whatever time you have to expand the velocity of your program, you can compose the bottleneck code stuck C and spot it into Python. I won't cover that in this book however you can take in more in the official Python documentation.)

Racks are like pickles with the exception of that they pickle items to an entrance by-key database, much like lexicons. Racks permit you to recreate an arbitrary access record or a database. It's not a genuine database but rather it frequently functions admirably enough for advancement and testing purposes.

Posting 10.8: Shelving information

```
>>>import s h e l v e #import s h e l v e l i b r a r y

>>>a _ l i s t = [ " one " , " two" , " clasp " ,
"my" , " shoe " ]
```

```
>>>dbase = shelve.open("filename")

>>>dbase["rhyme"] = a_list#save list under key name

>>>b_list = dbase["rhyme"]      #retrieve list
```

CHAPTER ELEVEN

STATEMENTS

Now that we know how Python uses its fundamental data types, let's talk about how to use them. Python is nominally a procedure-based language but as we'll see later, it also functions as an object-oriented language. As a matter of fact, it's similar to C++ in this aspect; you can use it as either a procedural or OO language or combine them as necessary.

The following is a listing of many Python statements. It's not all-inclusive but it gives you an idea of some of the features Python has.

Statement	*Role*	*Examples*
Assignment	Creatingreferences	new_car="Audi"
Calls	Runningfunctions	stdout.write("eggs, ham, toast\n")

Statement	*Role*	*Examples*
Print	Printingobjects	print"TheKiller",-joke
Print()	Python3.xprint-function	print("Haveyou-seenmy baseball?")
If/elif/else	Selectingactions	if"python"intex-t:print "yes"
For/else	Sequence iteration	forXin-mylist:printX
While/else	Generalloops	while1:print'hello'
Pass	Emptyplaceholder	while1:pass
Break,Continue	Loopjumps	while1:if not line:break
Try/except/fi-nally	Catchingexceptions	try:action() except: print'actionerror'
Raise	Triggerexception	raise locationError
Import,From	Moduleaccess	importsys;from-wx importwizard

Statement	Role	Examples
Def,Return	Buildingfunctions	deff(a,b,c=1,*d): retur- na+b+c+d[0]
Class	Buildingobjects	classsubclass:stat- icData =[]

11.1 Assignment

I've effectively discussed task some time recently. To repeat, task is fundamentally putting the objective name on the left of an equivalents sign and the item you're doling out to it on the privilege. There's just a couple of things you have to recall:

• Assignment makes article references.

• Assignment acts like pointers in C since it doesn't duplicate objects, just alludes to an article. Henceforth, you can have various assignments of the same article, i.e. a few unique names alluding to one item.

• Names are made when initially allocated

- Names don't need to be "predeclared"; Python makes the variable name when its initially made. Be that as it may, as you'll see, this doesn't mean you can approach a variable that hasn't been allocated an item yet. In the event that you call a name that hasn't been allotted yet, you'll get a special case mistake.

- Sometimes you may need to announce a name and give it a vacant worth, essentially as a "placeholder" for future use in your program. Case in point, in the event that you make a class to hold worldwide qualities, these worldwide qualities will be purge until another class utilizes them.

- Assignment can be made either the standard way (nourishment = "SPAM"), by means of numerous objective (spam = ham = "Yummy"), with a tuple (spam, ham = "lunch", "supper"), or with a rundown ([spam, ham] = ["blech", "YUM"]).

- This is another element that Python has over other languages. Numerous languages oblige you to have a different passage for every task, regardless of the fact that they are all going to have the same worth. With Python, you can continue adding names to the task articulation without making a different en- attempt every time.

The last thing to specify about task is that a name can be reassigned to distinctive articles. Since a name is only a reference to an item and doesn't need to be pronounced, you can change its "esteem" to anything. For instance:

Posting 11.1: Variable qualities aren't altered

```
>>>x = 0 #x is linked to an integer
>>>x = "spam" #now it"s a string
>>>x = [1, 2, 3] #now it"s a list
```

11.2   Expressions/Calls

Python expressions can be utilized as proclamations however since the outcome won't be spared, expressions are generally used to call capacities/ strategies and for printing qualities at the intuitive brief.

Here's the normal arrangement:

Posting 11.2: Expression samples

spam (eggs , ham) #function c a l utilizing enclosure spam . ham(eggs) #method c a l utilizing dab administrator spam #i n t e r a c t i v e p r i n t

spam < ham and ham != eggs   #c o m p o u n d expression

spam < ham < eggs #range t e s t

The extent test above gives you a chance to perform a Boolean test yet in a "nor- mal" design; it looks simply like an examination from math class. Once more, another helpful Python highlight that different languages don't fundamentally have.

11.3 Printing

Imprinting in Python is greatly basic. Utilizing print composes the yield to the C stdout stream and typically goes to the reassure unless you divert it to another document.

Presently is a decent time to say that Python has 3 streams for info/yield (I/O). sys.stdout is the standard yield stream; it is typically send to the screen however can be rerouted to a document or other area. sys.stdin is the standard info stream; it typically gets data from the console yet can likewise take information from a document or other area. sys.stderr is the standard blunder stream; it just takes mistakes from the program.

The print proclamation can be utilized with either the sys.stdout or sys.stderror streams. This permits you to augment proficiency. Case in point, you can print all program blunders to a log record and typical program yield to a printer or another program.

Printing, of course, includes a space between things isolated by commas and includes a linefeed toward the end of the yield stream. To smother the linefeed, simply include a comma toward the end of the print articulation:

Posting 11.3: Print illustration (no line sustain)

print logger , spam , eggs ,

To smother the space between components, simply link them when printing:

Posting 11.4: Printing linking

print " a" + "b"

Python 3.x replaces the basic print explanation with the print() capacity. This is to make it all the more capable, for example, permitting over-burdening, yet it requires almost no to change. As opposed to utilizing the print articulation like I have all through the book as such, you just allude to it as a capacity. Here are a few illustrations from the Python documentation page:

Old: print "The answer is", 2*2 New: print("The answer is", 2*2)

Old: print x, #Trailing comma stifles newline

New: print(x, end=" ") #Appends a space rather of a newline

Old: print #Prints a newline

New: print() #You must call the capacity!

Old: print >> sys.stderr, "deadly lapse" New: print("fatal blunder", file=sys.stderr)

Old: print (x, y) #prints repr((x, y))

New: print((x, y)) #Not the same as print(x, y)!

11.4 if Tests

A standout amongst the most widely recognized control structures you'll utilize, and keep running into in different programs, is the if contingent piece. Basically, you ask a yes or no inquiry; contingent upon the answer distinctive things happen. Case in point, you could say, "If the motion picture chose is 'The Meaning of Life', then print 'Great decision.' Otherwise, haphazardly select a film from the database."

In the event that you've programmed in different languages, the if articulation meets expectations the same as different languages. The main distinction is the else/if as demonstrated as follows:

Posting 11.5: Using if explanations

149

```
i f  thing == " magnet" :

k i t c h e n _ l i s t = [ " f r i d g e " ]

e l i f thing == " mirror " : #o p t i o n a l  condi-
tion

bathroom_ l i st = [ " s i n k " ]

e l i f thing == " growth " : #o p t i o n a l  con-
dition

l a n d s c a p e _ l i s t = [ " pink  f lamingo " ]

else : #o p t i o n a l  f i n a l  condition

print "No more cash to  redesign "
```

Having the elif (else/if) or the else articulation
isn't essential yet I like to have an else proclamation in my squares. It helps clear up to me what
the option is if the if condition isn't met. Also, later amendments can uproot it on the off chance
that its unessential.

Not at all like C, Pascal, and different languages,
there isn't a switch or case proclamation in Python. You can get the same usefulness by utilizing
if/elif tests, seeking records, or indexing lexicons.

Since records and word references are constructed at runtime, they can be more adaptable. Here's a comparable switch proclamation utilizing a lexicon:

Posting 11.6: Dictionary as a switch proclamation

```
>>>c h o i c e = 'ham "
>>>print { " spam " : 1 . 2 5 , #a d i c t i onary
–based " switch "
...      'ham " : 1 . 9 ,
...      ' eggs " : 0 . 9 ,
...      ' bacon " : 1 . 1 0 } [ c h o i c e ] 1 . 99
```

Clearly, this isn't the most natural approach to compose this program. A superior approach to do it is to make the lexicon as a different object, then utilize something like has_key() or generally discover the worth comparing to your decision.

Frankly, I don't consider along these lines of utilizing word references when I'm programming. It's not normal for me yet; despite everything I'm utilized to utilizing if/elif conditions. Once more, you can make your program utilizing if/elif proclamations and change them to word references or records when you update it. This can be a piece of typical refactoring (revising the code to make it simpler to oversee or read), some piece of bug chasing, or speed up.

11.5 while Loops

While circles (loops) are a standard workhorse of numerous languages. Basically, the program will keep doing something while a certain condition exists. When that condition is not more genuine, the circle stops.

The Python while articulation is, once more, like different languages.

Here's the primary organization:

Posting 11.7: while circles, section 1

while < t e s t >: #loop t e s t

<code block> #loop body

else : #o p t i o n a l e l s e s tatement

<code block> #run i f didn " t e x i t l oop with break

break and proceed with work literally the same as in C. What might as well be called C's unfilled articulation (a semicolon) is the pass proclamation, and Python incorporates an else explanation for utilization with breaks. Here's an all out while case circle:

while < t e s t >:

Posting 11.8: while circles, section 2

<statements>

i f < t e s t >: break #e x i t l oop now i f t regret

i f < t e s t >: proceed #return to top o f l oop now i f t regret

else :

<statements> # i f we didn " t h i t a " break "

break proclamations basically constrain the circle to stop early; when utilized with settled circles, it just leaves the littlest encasing circle. proceed proclamations cause the circle to begin once again, paying little respect to some other statements encourage on insider savvy. The else code piece is kept running "in transit out" of the circle, unless a break proclamation causes the circle to stop early. For the individuals who are still confounded, the following area will demonstrate how these announcements are utilized as a part of a true program with prime numbers.

11.6 For Loops

The for circle is an arrangement iterator for Python. It will take a shot at almost anything: strings, records, tuples, and so on. I've discussed for circles some time recently, and we will see a considerable measure of them in future parts, so I won't dive into a great deal more insight about them. The primary organization is beneath in Listing

11.9. Notice how it's basically the same as a while circle.

Posting 11.9: for circles

for <target > in <object >: #assign o b j e c t i tems to t a r g e t

<statements>

if <t e s t >: break #e x it l oop now , s k i p e l s e

if <t e s t >: proceed #go to top o f l oop now

else :

<statements> # i f we didn " t h it a " break "

From Learning Python from O'Reilly distributed:

"At the point when Python runs a for circle, it allocates things in the sequence article to the objective, one by one, and executes the circle body for each. The circle body normally utilizes the allocation focus to allude to the current thing in the succession, as if it were a cursor venturing through the grouping. Actually, the for works by over and again indexing the sequence question on progressively higher files (beginning at zero), until a list beyond the field of play special case is raised. Be-reason for circles consequently oversee arrangement indexing be- rear the scenes, they supplant the greater part of the counter style circles you may be accustomed to coding in languages like C."

As such, when the for circle begins, it takes a gander at the first thing in the rundown. This thing is given an estimation of 0 (numerous programming languages

begin tallying at 0, instead of 1). When the code square is done doing its handling, the for circle takes a gander at the second esteem and gives it an estimation of 1. Once more, the code piece does its preparing and the for circle takes a gander at the following quality and gives it an estimation of 2. This grouping proceeds until there are no more values in the rundown. By then the for circle stops and control continues to the following explanation in the program.

Posting 11.10 demonstrates a pragmatic adaptation of a for circle that implements break and else articulations, as clarified in the Python documentation.

Posting 11.10: break and else articulations

```
>>> for n in range ( 2 , 10 ):
...     for x in range ( 2 , n ):
...         if n % x == 0 :    # if the remaining portion of n/x is 0
...             print n , " parallels " , x ,      ' * " , n/x
...             break  #exit promptly
...     else :
...         # circle fel through without finding afactor
...         print n , " is a prime number "
...
2    is a prime number
3    is a prime number
4    equals 2 * 2
5    is a prime number
```

6   e q u a l s 2 * 3

7   i s a prime number

8   e q u a l s 2 * 4

9   e q u a l s 3 * 3

Identified with for circles are range and counter circles. The reach() capacity auto-constructs a rundown of numbers for you. Ordinarily its utilized to make files for a for explanation yet you can utilize it anyplace.

Posting 11.11: Using the reach() capacity

>>>r ange (5) #create a l i s t o f 5 numbers , s t a r t i n g at 0

[0 , 1 , 2 , 3 , 4]

>>>r ange (2 , 5) #s t a r t at 2 and end at 5 (recall the list values)

[2 , 3 , 4]

>>>r ange (0 , 10 , 2)   #s t a r t at 0 , end at 10 (list esteem) , with an increase o f 2

[0 , 2 , 4 , 6 , 8]

As should be obvious, a solitary contention gives you a rundown of whole numbers, beginning from 0 and closure at one not exactly the contention (in light of the list). Two contentions give a beginning number and the maximum quality while three contentions includes a going worth, i.e. what number of numbers to skip between every worth.

Counter circles essentially tally the quantity of times the circle has been prepared. Toward the end of the circle, a variable is augmented to demonstrate that the circle has been finished. When a specific number of circles have happened, the circle is executed and whatever is left of the program is executed.

11.7   pass Statement

The pass explanation is essentially an approach to advise Python to proceed moving, nothing to see here. Regularly, the pass articulation is utilized while at first composition a program. You may make a reference to a function however haven't really actualized any code for it yet. In any case, Python will be searching for something inside of that capacity. Without having something to process, the Python translator will give an exception and stop when it doesn't discover anything. In the event that you essentially put a pass proclamation in the capacity, it will proceed without halting.

Posting 11.12: pass articulations

```
if variable > 12:
```

print "Better believe it, that " s a huge number . "

else : pass

11.8   break and proceed with Statements

Officially specified, these two announcements influence the stream control inside a circle. At the point when a specific condition is met, the break explanation "breaks" unaware of what's going on, successfully finishing the circle rashly (however in a normal way). Then proceed with articulation "shortcircuits" the circle, bringing about stream control to come back to the highest point of the circle quickly.

I infrequently utilize these announcements yet they respect have when required. They help guarantee you don't get stuck in a circle always furthermore guarantee that you don't continue emphasizing through the circle for reasons unknown.

11.9 Try, aside from, at last and raise Statements

I've quickly touched on some of these and will discuss them all the more in the Exceptions section. Quickly, attempt makes a square that endeavors to perform an activity. On the off chance that that activity comes up short with the exception of piece gets any exemption that is raised and makes a move, at long last performs some spur of the moment activities, paying little respect to whether a special case was raised or not. The raise explanation physically makes an exemption.

11.10 import and from Statements

These two announcements are utilized to incorporate other Python libraries and modules that you need to use in your program. This serves to keep your program little (you don't need to put all the code inside of a solitary module) and "separates" modules (you just import what you require). import really calls alternate libraries or modules while from puts forth the import expression particular; you just import subsections of a module, minimizing the measure of code brought into your program.

11.11 def and return Statements

These are utilized as a part of capacities and methods.   Functions are utilized as a part of procedural-based programming while strategies are utilized as a part of item arranged

programming. The def articulation characterizes the capacity/strategy. The arrival explanation gives back a quality from the capacity or strategy, permitting you to dole out the returned worth to a variable.

```
>>> a = 2

>>> b = 5
```

Posting 11.13: Defining capacities

```
>>> def math_function ( ) :
...     return  a  *  b
...
>>> item = math_function ( )
>>>  item 10
```

11.12 Class Statements

These are the building pieces of OOP. class makes another article. This article can be anything, whether a conceptual information idea or a model of a physical item, e.g. a seat. Every class has individual character- istics extraordinary to that class, including variables and routines. Classes are intense and at present "the huge thing" in most programming languages. Thus, there are a few sections committed to OOP later in books.

CHAPTER TWELVE

DOCUMENTING YOUR CODE

Some of this data is obtained from Dive Into Python, a free Python programming book for experienced programmers. Other data is from the Python Style Guide and the Python Enhancement Proposal (PEP) 257. (Note that in this area, the data introduced may be as opposed to the official Python guides. This data is displayed in a general configuration in regards to docstrings and uses the traditions that I have created. The peruser is urged to survey the official documentation for further subtle elements.)

You can record a Python question by giving it a docstring. A docstring is just a triple-cited sentence giving a brief synopsis of the item. The article can be a capacity, system, class, and so forth. (In this area, the expression "capacity" is utilized to imply a genuine capacity or a technique, class, or other Python object.)

Posting 12.1: docstring illustration

def b u i l d C o n e c t i o n S t r i n g (params) :

""" Build a association s t r i n g from a d i c t i o n a r y o f parameters .

Returns s t r i n g . """

As noted already, triple quotes connote a multi-line string. Ev- erything between the begin and end quotes is a piece of a solitary string, including carriage returns and other quote characters. You'll see them frequently utilized when characterizing a docstring.

Everything between the triple quotes is the capacity's docstring, which reports what the capacity does. A docstring, in the event that it exists, must be the first thing characterized in a capacity (that is, the first thing after the colon).

You don't in fact need to give your capacity a docstring, yet you ought to; the docstring is accessible at runtime as a quality of the capacity. Numerous Python IDEs utilize the docstring to give connection touchy documentation, so that when you write a capacity name, its docstring shows up as a tooltip.

From the Python Style Guide:

"The docstring of a script ought to be usable as its "use" message, printed when the script is conjured with incorrect or missing contentions (or maybe with a "-h" choice, for "help"). Such a docstring ought to archive the script's capacity and summon line punctuation, environment variables, and records. Utilization messages can be genuinely expound (a few screenfuls) and ought to be adequate for another client to utilize the order appropriately, and also a complete snappy reference to all alternatives and contentions for the advanced client."

Frankly, I don't stick to this manage constantly. I regularly compose a short articulation about what the capacity, system, class, and so on should achieve. On the other hand, as my programs advance I attempt to upgrade the docstring, including what inputs it gets and what the yield is, if any.

There are two types of docstrings: one-liners and multi-line doc- strings. One-liners are precisely that: data that needn't bother with a ton of enlightening content to clarify what's going on. Triple quotes are utilized despite the fact that the string fits on one line to make it simple to later grow it. The end quotes are on the same line as the opening quotes, since it looks better. There's no clear line either before or after the docstring. The docstring is an expression finishing in a period. It portrays the capacity's impact as a charge ("Do this", "Arrival that"). It ought not restate the capacity's parameters (or contentions) but rather it can express the normal return esteem, if present.

Posting 12.2: Good utilization of docstring def kos_ root ( ) :

"""" Return the pathname o f the KOS root d i rectory."""global _kos_root

if _kos_root: re t ur n _kos_root

. . .

Once more, I need to concede I'm not the best about this. I typically put the end cites on a different line and I have a space between the docstring and the begin of the real code; it makes it less demanding to just add data and serves to outline the docstring from whatever remains of the code piece. Yes, I'm an awful individual. In any case, the length of you are predictable all through your undertakings, blind adherence to "the Python way" isn't essential.

As a side note, it's not absolutely wrong to have the end cites on a different line; the multi-line docstring ought to (as indicated by PEP 257) have them that way while an one-line docstring ought to have the end cites on the same line. I've recently gotten in the propensity for utilizing one strategy when composing my docstrings so I don't need to consider it. Multi-line docstrings begin simply like a solitary line docstring. The principal line is a synopsis however is then trailed by a clear line. After the clear line more enlightening discourse can be made. The clear line is utilized to partitioned the rundown from engaging information for automatic indexing apparatuses. They will utilize the one-line synopsis to make a documentation list, permitting the programmer to do less work.

At the point when proceeding with your docstring after the clear line, make a point to take after the space rules for Python, i.e. after the clear line the majority of your docstring data is indented similarly as the beginning triple-cite. Else you will get mistakes when you run your program.

More data from the Python Style Guide:

"The docstring for a module ought to by and large rundown the classes, exemptions and capacities (and some other articles) that are sent out by the module, with an one-line synopsis of each. (These synopses by and large give less detail than the total mary line in the object's docstring.)"

The docstring for a capacity or technique ought to outline its conduct and archive its contentions, return value(s), symptoms, exemptions raised, and confinements on when it can be called (all if relevant). Discretionary contentions ought to be demonstrated. It ought to be reported whether essential word contentions are a piece of the interface.

The docstring for a class ought to abridge its conduct and rundown people in general routines and example variables. On the off chance that the class is proposed to be subclassed, and thought an extra interface for subclasses, this interface to be recorded independently (in the docstring). The class constructor ought to be reported in the docstring for its init strategy (the "introduction" system that is conjured when the class is initially called). Singular routines ought to be archived by their own docstring.

In the event that a class subclasses another class and its conduct is generally inherited from that class, its docstring ought to say this and compress the distinctions. Utilize the verb "override" to show that a subclass system replaces a superclass strategy and does not call the superclass technique; utilize the verb "reach out" to demonstrate that a subclass strategy calls the superclass system (notwithstanding its own particular conduct).

Python is case touchy and the contention names can be utilized for watchword contentions, so the docstring ought to record the right argument names. It is best to rundown every contention on a different line, with two dashes isolating the name from the portrayal

In the event that you've made it this far, I'll bail you out and compress what you simply realized. Python has a documentation highlight called "docstring" that permits you to utilize remarks to make self-reporting source code. A few Python IDEs, for example, Stani's Python Editor (SPE), can utilize these docstrings to make a posting of your source code structures, for example, classes and modules. This makes it less demanding on the programmer since less work is obliged when you make your help records and other program documentation. Documentation indexers can pull the doc- strings out of your code and make a posting for you, or you could even make your own particular script to make it for you. You are additionally ready to manually read the docstrings of articles by calling the doc system for an item; this is basically what the above IDEs and indexers are doing. Posting 12.3 shows how a docstring for Python's irregular module.

Posting 12.3: docstring for Python's arbitrary module

>>>i mport arbitrary

>>>p r i n t arbitrary .   doc   Random v a r
i a b l e g e n e r a t o r s .

i n t e g e r s

----

uniform inside range

arrangements

----

pick arbitrary component pick irregular specimen

g e n e r a t e arbitrary stage

d i s t r i b u t i o n s on the r e a l l i n e :

_____

uniform

t r i a n g u l a r

typical (Gaussian) lognormal

n e g a t i v e e x p o n e n t i a l gamma

beta pareto Weibull

d i s t r i b u t i o n s on the c i r c l e (a n g l e s
o to 2 pi)

_____
_____

c i r c u l a r uniform von Mises

General notes on the basic Mersenne Twister
center g e n e r a t o r :

* The p e r i o d i s $2^{**}19937 - 1$.

* I t i s one o f the most e x t e n s i v e l y t e s

t e d g e n e r a t o r s in e x i s t e n c e .

*Withouta direct waytocomputeN steps
    forward,thesemantics of jumpa-
    head(n) areweakenedtosimplyjump-
    toanotherdistant state andrely

    onthelarge   period
    toavoidoverlappingsequenc-
    es.

*Therandom() methodis implementedinC,

    executes ina single Pythonstep,
    andis,therefore, threadsafe.

This doesn't really tell you everything you
need to know about the module; this is simply
the description of the *random* module. To get a
comprehensive listing of the module, you would
have to type *"help(random)"* at the Python inter-
preter prompt. Doing this will give you 22pages
of formatted text, similar to*nix*man*pages, that
will tell you everything you need to know about
the module.

Alternatively, if you only want to know the functions a module provides, you can use the **dir()** function, as shown in Listing12.4.

Listing12.4:Functions for *random* module

>>>dir(random)

['BPF', 'LOG4', 'NV_MAGICCONST', 'RECIP_BPF', 'Random', 'SG_MAGIC-CONST',

'SystemRandom', 'TWOPI', 'WichmannHill', '

_BuiltinMethodType', '_MethodType',

'__all__', '__builtins__', '__doc__', '__file__','____name____', 'package___ ', '

'_acos', '_ceil', '_cos', '_e', '_exp', '_hexlify', '_inst', '_log', '_pi',

'_random', '_sin', '_sqrt', '_test', '

_test_generator', '_urandom', '_warn',

'betavariate', 'choice', 'division', 'expo-
variate', 'gammavariate', 'gauss',

'getrandbits', 'getstate', 'jumpahead ', 'log-
normvariate' , 'normalvariate' ,

'paretovariate', 'randint', 'random', 'ran-
drange','sample', 'seed', 'setstate',

'shuffle', 'triangular', 'uniform', 'vonmis-
esvariate', 'weibullvariate']

Naturally, the only way to harness the power of doc strings is to follow the style rules Python expects, meaning you have to use triple-quotes, separate your summary line from the full-blown description, etc. You can document your Python code without following these rules but then it's up to you to create a help file or whatever. I haven't had any problems with my doc strings yet but only because I slightly modify how they are formatted (having a space between the doc string and code, putting end quotes on a separate line, etc.)Be careful if you desire to not follow the Style Guide.

Not only will it make your life easier when you finish your project, but it also makes your code easier to read and follow. (Wish the people at my work could learn how to document their code. Even just a few comments explaining what a function does would help.

CHAPTER THIRTEEN

MAKING A PROGRAM

In the wake of having utilized it for a long time now, I've come to find that Python is an amazingly able language, meet in energy to C++, Java, et al. On the off chance that you needn't bother with the "artfulness" the significant languages give, I profoundly suggest learning Python or another element language like Ruby. You'll program quicker with less slips (like memory administration) and can tackle the force of an inherent GUI for quick prototyping of utilizations. You can likewise utilize these languages for fast scripts to speed monotonous errands. In addition, they are innately cross-stage so you can without much of a stretch switch between operating systems or locate a bigger business sector for your programs. Hell, Python is utilized widely by Google, NASA, and numerous diversion distributers, so it can't be all that awful.

One of the greatest dissentions individuals have is the constrained utilization of white space and space. However, in the event that you consider it, which is viewed as a "decent coding practice"; it makes it less demanding to take after the stream of the program and lessens the shot of lapses. In addition, since sections aren't obliged, you don't need to stress over your program not living up to expectations in light of the fact that you neglected to close a settled if articulation. Following a couple of days of utilizing Python, you won't even notice, however I envision you'll see how "messy" different languages look.

Presently, on with the show...

13.1   Making Python Do Something

So far I've discussed how Python is organized and how it varies from different languages. Presently now is the right time to make some genuine programs. In the first place, Python programs are involved capacities, classes, modules, and bundles.

1. Functions are programmer made code hinders that do a particular undertaking.

2. Classes are article situated structures that I'll discuss later; suffice to say they are really capable structures that can make programming life simpler, however they can be hard to learn and wield well.

3. Modules are by and large thought to be ordinary program documents, i.e. a document included capacities/classes, circles, control explanations, and so forth.

4. Packages are programs comprised of a wide range of modules.

In all actuality, I consider modules and bundles to be "programs". It just relies on upon what number of particular records is obliged to make the program run. Yes, it is conceivable to have a solitary, solid document that controls the whole program however its normally better to have diverse parts in distinctive documents. It's really less demanding to stay informed concerning what's going on and you can group bits of code that have normal objectives, e.g. have a record that holds library works, one that handles the GUI, and one that procedures information passage.

An imperative module to know is the Python standard library. There are two adaptations: Python 2.6 and Python 3.0. The library is an accumulation of normal code obstructs that you can call when required. This implies you don't need to "modify the wheel" each time you need to do something, for example, compute the digression of a capacity. You should simply import the bit of the standard library you require, e.g. the math square, and afterward utilize it like standard Python code. Comprehending what's in the standard library isolates the great programmers from the immense ones, at any rate in my book.

That being said, we should make a straightforward Python program. This genius gram can be made in IDLE (the standard Python programming environment that accompanies the Python introduce), an outsider programming environment, (for example, SPE, Komodo, Eclipse, BoaConstructor, and so on.), or a basic content manager like Window's Notepad, vim, emacs, BBE- dit, and so on. (More programs can be found in the supplement on page 168).

Posting 13.1: First illustration program

```
def square ( x ) :    #define the f unction ; " x"
i s  the contention

return x * x #pass back to c a l e r the square
o f a number

for y in range ( 1 , 11 ) :    #c y c l e through a l
i s t o f numbers

print square ( y ) #p r i n t the square o f a
number
```

Posting 13.1 is about more or less basic. In the first place we characterize the capacity called square() (the enclosure shows that it's a capacity instead of an announcement) and let it know that the contention called "x" will be utilized for handling. At that point we really characterize what the capacity will do; for this situation, it will increase "x" times itself to create a square. By utilizing the magic word give back, the square esteem will be offered back to whatever really called the capacity (for this situation, the print explanation).

Next we make a for circle that prints the squared estimation of every number as it increments from 1 to 11. This ought to be genuinely simple to take after, particularly with the remarks off to the side. Understand that numerous programs you'll see aren't remarked this much; all the time, the programs aren't remarked by any means. I like to imagine that I have an adequate measure of documentation in my code (you'll see later) so it's really simple for even new programmers to make sense of what's going on.

To run this program, basically spare it with a filename, for example, "first_program.py".

At that point, at the summon provoke essentially sort "python first_program.py". The outcomes ought to resemble this:

Posting 13.2: First illustration program yield

```
$python f i rst_ program . py        #your  charge
provoke by  d i f e r  from  "$"
```

1

4

9

16

25

36

49

64

81

100

How about we take a gander at another program, this one somewhat more perplexing?

Posting 13.3: Second sample program and yield

```
def viper ( * args ) :  #accept m u l t i p l e con-
tentions

aggregate = args [ 0 ]      #create a b l ank l i s
t

for next in args [ 1 : ] :  #i t e r a t e through
contentions

aggregate = total + next   #add contentions

return aggregate

>>> viper ( 2 , 3 )

5

>>> viper ( 4 , 5 , 56 )

65

>>> viper ( "spam" , " eggs " ) " spameggs "

>>> viper ( [ 1 , 2 , 3 ] , [ 4 , 5 , 6 ] )

[ 1 , 2 , 3 , 4 , 5 , 6 ]
```

This little program is really capable, as should be obvious. Basically, it takes a variable number of contentions and either includes them or con- catenates them together, contingent upon the contention sort. These contentions can be anything: numbers, strings, records, tuples, and so on.

A note about the *args pivotal word. This is an uncommon element of Python that permits you to enter undesignated contentions and do things to them (like include them together). The "*" is similar to a special case; it means that a variable number of contentions can be given. A comparable contention catchphrase is **kwargs. This one is connected (it takes a boundless number of contentions) yet the contentions are situated off by essential words. Along these lines, you can coordinate variables to the contentions taking into account the catchphrases. More data can be found in Section 13.3 (Default Arguments) underneath.

13.2 Scope

What? You didn't know snakes got terrible breath? (I know, terrible joke.) Seriously however, extension depicts the region of a program where an iden- tifier (a name for something, similar to a variable) can get to its related quality. Degree ties in with namespaces in light of the fact that name-spaces essentially characterize where an identifi-er's extension is.

In straightforward terms, namespaces store data around an identifier and its esteem. Python has three namespaces: neighborhood, worldwide, and manufactured in. At the point when an identifier is initially gotten to, Python searches for its esteem mainly, i.e. its encompassing code piece. In the il-lustration above, "x" is characterized inside of the capacity square(). Each capacity is appointed its own nearby namespace. Capacities can't utilize identifiers characterized in different capacities; they're just not seen. In the event that a capaci-ty tries to call a variable characterized in another capacity, you'll get a lapse. On the off chance that a capacity attempted to characterize a formerly characterized variable, you'll simply get a shiny new variable that happens to have the same name yet an alternate worth.

Then again, if an identifier isn't characterized pro-vincially, Python will weigh in the event that it's in the worldwide namespace. The worldwide namespace is not the same as the neighborhood one in that worldwide identifiers can be utilized by different capacities. So on the off chance that you made worldwide variable cars_in_shop = 2, all capacities in the program can get to that variable and utilization it as required. So you can characterize a variable in one area and have it utilized as a part of various spots without needing to make it again and again. Be that as it may, this isn't prescribed on the grounds that it can prompt security issues or programming issues. Case in point, making a variable worldwide means any capacity can get to them. On the off chance that you begin having various capacities utilizing the same variable, you don't comprehend what is going on to the variable at any given time; there is no ensure its esteem will be what you anticipate that it will be the point at which you utilize it.

This isn't to say that worldwide variables are a strict no-no. They are helpful and can make your life simpler, when utilized properly. Yet, they can constrain the adaptability of a program and regularly prompt unexplained rationale slips, so I have a tendency to stay far from them.

The implicit namespace is situated aside for Python's inherent capacities. (Kinda helpful, huh?) So magic words and standard capacity calls like extent() are now characterized when the Python mediator begins up and you can utilize them "out of the container".

As you may have made sense of, namespaces are settled: fabricated in

'*   global

'*   local

On the off chance that an identifier isn't discovered generally, Python will check the worldwide namespace. In the event that it's not there Python will check the implicit namespace. On the off chance that it still can't discover it, it hacks up a lapse and kicks the bucket.

One thing to consider (and I touched on marginally) is that you can conceal identifiers as you go down the namespace tree. In the event that you have cars_in_shop = 2 characterized all around, you can make a capacity that has literally the same name with an alternate quality, e.g. cars_in_shop = 15. At the point when the capacity calls this variable, it will utilize the estimation of 15 versus 2 to figure the outcome. This is another issue of worldwide variables; they can bring about issues on the off chance that you don't have great variable names since you may overlook which variable you're really using.

13.3   Default Arguments

When you make a capacity, you can set it up to utilize default values for its contentions, just in the event that the thing calling it doesn't have any contentions. Case in point:

Posting 13.4: Default contentions

```
def edge ( l e n g t h = 1 , width = 1 ) :

return l e n g t h * width
```

On the off chance that you need to call this specific capacity, you can supply it with the essential estimations [perimeter(15, 25)] or you can supply one [perimeter(7)] or you can simply utilize the defaults [perimeter()]. Every contention is coordinated to the went in qualities, all together, so in case you're going to do this verify you know which contentions will be coordinated, i.e. in the event that you supply only one contention, it will supplant the first default esteem however some other qualities will stay as defaults.

You can likewise utilize catchphrase contentions, which coordinate contentions in light of a comparing decisive word. Along these lines, you don't need to stress over the request they are given. So for the "edge()" case above, you could just say "perimeter(width = 12)". This will make the capacity utilize 1 for the length and 12 for the width. This is less demanding than recalling the request of the contentions; be that as it may, it additionally implies all the more writing for you. On the off chance that you have a great deal of capacities with these sorts of contentions, it can get to be monotonous.

Moreover, once you give a pivotal word for a contention, you can't backtrack to not naming them then attempt to depend on position to show the matchup. For instance:

Posting 13.5: Default contentions and position

```
def a b s t r a c t _ f u n c t i o n ( c o l o r = " blue
" , s i z e = 30 , range = 40 ,  noodle = True ) :

pass

#c a l  the  f unction

a b s t r a c t _ f u n c t i o n ( " red " ,  noodle =
False ,  45 ,  range

= 50 ) #not  a l owed
```

Attempting it call it along these lines will give you a blunder. When you begin utilizing pivotal words, you need to proceed for whatever is left of the contention set. That is about it for programming with capacities. They're really basic and the more samples you see, the more they'll bode well. Python is cool since you can blend capacities and classes (with routines) in the same module without agonizing over mistakes. Thusly you aren't compelled to one method for programming; if a short capacity will work, you don't need to take the time to make an all-out class with a strategy to do likewise.

In the event that you would prefer not to manage item situated programming, you can stay with capacities and have a decent time. Then again, I'll begin to cover OOP in later parts to demonstrate to you why it's great to know and utilization. Furthermore, with Python, it's not as alarming as OOP execution in different language.

CHAPTER FOURTEEN

EXCEPTIONS

I've discussed special cases before however now I will discuss them inside and out. Basically, special cases are occasions that change program's stream, either deliberately or because of blunders. They are extraordinary occasions that can happen because of a slip, e.g. attempting to open a document that doesn't exist, or when the program achieves a marker, for example, the finish of a circle. Exemptions, by definition, don't happen frequently; consequently, they are the "special case to the principle" and an extraordinary class has been made for them. Exemptions are all over in Python. For all intents and purposes each module in the standard Python library utilizes them, and Python itself will bring them up in various circumstances. Here are only a couple of cases:

- Accessing a non–existent word reference key will raise a KeyError exemption.

- Searching a rundown for a non–existent quality will raise a ValueError exemption.

- Calling a non–existent system will raise an AttributeError ex- ception.

- Referencing a non–existent variable will raise a NameError ex- ception.

- Mixing datatypes without pressure will raise a TypeError excep- tion.

One utilization of exemptions is to catch an issue and permit the program to keep working; we have seen this before when we discussed documents. This is the most widely recognized approach to utilize special cases. At the point when programming with the Python charge line translator, you don't have to stress over getting exemptions. Your program is normally sufficiently short to not be hurt an excess of if an exemption happens. Also, having the excep- tion happen at the charge line is a speedy and simple approach to tell if your code rationale has an issue. Then again, if the same slip happened in your genuine program, it will come up short and quit working.

Special cases can be made physically in the code by raising an ex- ception. It works precisely as a system-created special cases, with the exception of that the programmer is doing it deliberately. This can be for various reasons. One of the advantages of utilizing special cases is that, by their temperament, they don't put any overhead on the code preparing. Since exemptions should happen regularly, they aren't handled until they happen.

Special cases can be considered as an extraordinary type of the if/elif statements. You can sensibly do likewise with if obstructs as you can with exemptions. In any case, as effectively specified, exemptions aren't prepared until they happen; if pieces are handled constantly. Legitimate utilization of special cases can help the execution of your program. The more occasional the lapse may happen the better off you are to utilize exceptions; utilizing if squares obliges Python to constantly test additional conditions before proceeding. Exemptions likewise make code administration simpler: if your programming rationale is blended in with mistake taking care of if articulations, it can be hard to peruse, alter, and investigate your program.

Here is a straightforward program that highlights the greater part of the critical components of exemption preparing. It just creates the remainder of 2 numbers.

Posting 14.1: Exceptions

f irst_ number = raw_input (" Enter the f i r s t number . "

) #g e t s info from console

sec_number = raw_input (" Enter the second number . ")

attempt :

num1 = f l o a t (f irst_ number) num2 = f l o a t (sec_number)

r e s u l t = num1/num2

but Value Error :   #not enough numbers entered

print "Two numbers will be r e q u i r e d . "

but Z e r o D i v i s i o n E r o r :   #t r i e d to d i v i d e by 0

print " Zero can " t be a denominator . "

else :

print s t r (num1) + "/" + s t r (num2) + "=" + s t r (r e s u l t)

#a l t e r n a t i v e position

#a t u p l e is r equired f or m u l t i p l e values

#printed values have f l o a t i n g numbers with one decimal point

print "%.1 f/%.1 f =%.1 f " % (num1 , num2 , r e s u l t)

As should be obvious, you can have a few "special case catchers" in the same attempt square. You can likewise utilize the else articulation toward the end to signify the rationale to perform if all goes well; in any case, it's a bit much. As expressed some time recently, the entire attempt piece could likewise have been composed as though/elif articulations however that would have obliged Python to process every announcement to check whether they coordinated. By utilizing special cases, the "default" case is thought to be valid until an exemption really happens. These rates up preparing.

One change you could make to this program is to just put it all inside of the attempt square. The raw_input() variables (which catch information from the client's console) could be put inside of the attempt piece, supplanting the "num1" and "num2" variables by driving the client info to a buoy worth, similar to so: attempt :

Posting 14.2: User data with attempt explanations

numerator = f l o a t (raw_input (" Enter the numerator . ")

denominator = f l o a t (raw_input (" Enter the denominator . ")

Thusly, you lessen the measure of rationale that must be composed, handled, and tried. Despite everything you have the same exemptions; you're simply streamlining the program.

At last, it's ideal to incorporate mistake checking, for example, special cases, in your code as you program as opposed to as an idea in retrospect. An exceptional "classification" of programming includes composing experiments to guarantee that most conceivable blunders are represented in the code, particularly as the code changes or new forms are made. By arranging ahead and putting special cases and other lapse registering code with your program at the beginning, you guarantee that issues are gotten before they can bring about issues. By overhauling your experiments as your program advances, you guarantee that form rede-signs keep up similarity and a fix doesn't make a blunder condition.

14.1   Exception Class Hierarchy

Table 14.1 demonstrates the chain of importance of special cases from the Python Library Reference. At the point when an exemption happens, it begins at the least level conceivable (a tyke) and voyages upward (through the folks), holding up to be gotten. This implies two or three things to a programmer:

1. If you don't recognize what special case may happen, you can simply get a more elevated amount exemption. Case in point, on the off chance that you didn't realize that ZeroDivisionError from the past illustration was a "stand-alone" exemption, you could have utilized the ArithmeticError for the exemption and got that; as the graph demonstrates, ZeroDivisionError is an offspring of ArithmeticError, which thusly is an offspring of StandardError, thus on up the progressive system.

2. Multiple special cases can be dealt with the same way. Taking after on with the above

sample, assume you anticipate utilizing the ZeroDivisionError and you need to incorporate the FloatingPointError. On the off chance that you needed to have the same move made for both mistakes, sim- utilize the guardian exemption ArithmeticError as the special case to catch. That way, when either a coasting point or zero division slip happens, you don't need to have a different case for everyone. Actually, on the off chance that you have a need or craving to catch every one separately, maybe on the grounds that you need diverse moves to be made, then written work exemptions for every case is fine.

BaseException

+− SystemExit

Table 14.1: Exception Hierarchy

+− KeyboardInterrupt

+− GeneratorExit

+− Exception

+− StopIteration

+– StandardError

| +– BufferError

| +– ArithmeticError

| | +– FloatingPointError

| | +– OverflowError

| | +– ZeroDivisionError

| +– AssertionError

| +– AttributeError

| +– EnvironmentError

| | +– IOError

| | +– OSError

| | +– WindowsError (Windows)

| | +– VMSError (VMS)

| +– EOFError

| +– ImportError

| +– LookupError

| | +– IndexError

| | +– KeyError

| +– MemoryError

| +– NameError

| | +– UnboundLocalError

| +– ReferenceError

| +– RuntimeError

| | +– NotImplementedError

| +– SyntaxError

| | +– IndentationError

| | +– TabError

| +– SystemError

| +– TypeError

| +– ValueError

| +– UnicodeError

 |+–UnicodeTranslateError

 +–Warnings(various)

1.1   User-Defi Exceptions

I won't spend too much time talking about this, but Python does allow for a programmer to create his own exceptions. You probably won't have to do this very often but it's nice to have the option when necessary. However, before making your own exceptions, make sure there isn't one of the built-in exceptions that will work for you. They have been "testedbyfire" over the years and not only work effectively, they have been optimized for performance and a rebug-free.

Making your own exceptions involves object-oriented programming, which will be covered in the next chapter. To make a custom exception, the programmer determines which base exception to use as the class to inherit from, e.g. making an exception for negative numbers or one for imaginary numbers would probably fall under the ArithmeticError exception class. To make a custom exception, simply inherit the base exception and define what it will do. Listing14.3 gives an example of creating a custom exception:

Listing 14.3: Defining custom exceptions

importmath#*necessaryforsquareroot-function*

classNegativeNumberError(Arithmetic-

Error):

"""Attemptedimproperoperation on-negative number

. *""""*

pass

defsquareRoot(number):

"""Computessquarerootof number. RaisesNega-tiveNumberError

if numberis less than0."""

if number<0:

raiseNegativeNumberError , \

"Squarerootof negative numbernotpermitted"

returnmath.sqrt(number)

The first line creates the custom exception Negative Number Error, which inherits from Arithmetic Error. Because it inherits all the features of the base exception, you don't have to define anything else, hence the pass statement that signifies that no actions are to be performed. Then, to use the new exception, a function is created (**squareRoot()**) that calls NegativeNumberError if the argument value is less than 0, otherwise it gives the square root of the number.

CHAPTER FIFTEEN

OBJECT ORIENTED PROGRAMMING

1.1   Learning Python Classes

The class is the most essential part of article situated programming. Already, you figured out how to utilize capacities to make your program do something. Presently, will move into the huge, terrifying universe of Object-Oriented Programming (OOP).

In all honesty, it took me a while to understand objects. When I initially learned C and C++, I did extraordinary; works simply appeared well and good for me. Having messed around with BASIC in the mid '90s, I understood capacities were much the same as subroutines so there wasn't much new to learn. Nonetheless, when my C++ course began discussing questions, classes, and

209

all the new components of OOP, my evaluations certainly endured.

When you learn OOP, you'll understand that it's really a lovely powerful instrument. In addition numerous Python libraries and APIs utilization classes, so you ought to in any event have the capacity to comprehend what the code is doing.

One thing to note about Python and OOP: it's not required to utilize protests in your code. As you've as of now seen, Python can do fine and dandy with capacities. Dissimilar to languages, for example, Java, you aren't secured to a solitary method for doing things; you can blend capacities and classes as vital in the same program. This gives you a chance to fabricate the code

111

in a manner that works best; perhaps you don't have to have an all out class with introduction code and routines to simply give back a computation. With Python, you can get as specialized as you need.

15.2   How are Classes Better?

Envision you have a program that ascertains the speed of an auto in a two-dimensional plane utilizing capacities. On the off chance that you need to make another program that ascertains the speed of a plane in three measurements, you can utilize the ideas of your auto capacities to make the plane model work, however you'll need to rework the a large portion of the capacities to make them work for the vertical measurement, particularly need to guide the item in a 3-D space. You may be fortunate and have the capacity to duplicate and glue some of them, however generally you'll need to retry a great part of the work.

Classes let you characterize an item once, then reuse it different times. You can give it a base capacity (called a strategy in OOP speech) then expand upon that system to reclassify it as important. It likewise gives you a chance to model true protests vastly improved than utilizing capacities.

Case in point, you could make a tire class that characterizes the measure of the tire, the amount of weight it holds, what it's made of, and so forth then make strategies to decide how rapidly it wears out taking into account certain conditions. You can then utilize this tire class as a component of an auto class, a bike class, or whatever. Every utilization of the tire class (called cases) would utilize distinctive properties of the base tire object. In the event that the base tire item said it was simply made of elastic, maybe the auto class would "improve" the tire by saying it had steel groups or perhaps the bicycle class would say it has an inside air bladder. This will bode well later.

15.3   Improving Your Class Standing

A few ideas of classes are critical to know.

1. Classes have a positive namespace, much the same as modules. Attempting to call a class technique from an alternate class will give you a slip unless you qualify it, e.g. spamClass. eggMethod().

2. Classes bolster different duplicates. This is on account of classes have two distinct articles:

class protests and occurrence objects. Class items give the default conduct and are utilized to make occasion objects. Case items are the articles that really take the necessary steps in your program. You can have the same number of occurrence objects of the same class protest as you need. Example articles are normally checked by the magic word self, so a class system could be Car.Brake() while a particular occurrence of the Brake() technique would be stamped as self.Brake(). (I'll cover this in more profundity later).

3. Each example item has its own particular namespace additionally acquires from the base class object. This implies every occurrence has the same default namespace segments as the class object, yet notice ditionally every example can make new namespace protests only for itself.

4. Classes can characterize objects that react to the same operations as implicit sorts. So class articles can be cut, listed, concatenated,

and so forth simply like strings, records, and other standard Python sorts. This is on account of everything in Python is really a class object; we aren't really doing anything new with classes, we're simply figuring out how to better utilize the intrinsic way of the Python language.

Here's a brief rundown of Python OOP thoughts:

- The class articulation makes a class question and gives it a name. This makes another namespace.

- Assignments inside of the class make class properties. These at- tributes are gotten to by qualifying the name utilizing dab sentence structure: ClassName.Attribute.

- Class properties trade the condition of an item and its related conduct. These traits are shared by all cases of a class.

- Calling a class (simply like a capacity) makes another occasion of the class. This is the place the different duplicates part comes in.

- Each occasion gets ("acquires") the default class qualities and gets its own namespace. This keeps example objects from covering and befuddling the program.

- Using the term self recognizes a specific occasion, considering per-occurrence qualities. This permits things, for example, variables to be connected with a specif instance

15.4 So What Does a Class Look Like?

Before we leave this specific instructional exercise, I'll give you some snappy examples to clarify what I've discussed as such. Expecting your utilizing the Python intuitive mediator, here's the way a straightforward class would resemble.

Posting 15.1: Defining a class

```
>>> class Hero : #define a c l a s o b j e c t

...          def setName ( s e l f , esteem ) :
#define c l a s techniques

...          s e l f . name = value #s e l f i d e n
tifies a particular example
```

```
...    def display(self):

...          print self.name #print the in-
```
formation f or a p a r t i c u l a r example

There are a couple of things to notice about this case:

1. When the class article is characterized, there are no enclosure toward the end; bracket are utilized for capacities and techniques. On the other hand, see Section 15.5 for an admonition.

2. The first contention in the enclosures for a class technique must act naturally. This is utilized to distinguish the example calling the technique. The Python mediator handles the calls inside. You should simply verify self is the place it should be so you don't get a lapse. Despite the fact that you must utilize self to recognize every example, Python is sufficiently brilliant to know which specific in- position is being referenced, so having numerous occasions in the meantime is not an issue. (self

is like this, which is utilized as a part of a few different languages like Java).

3. When you are relegating variables, as "self. name", the variable must be qualified with the "self" title. Once more, this is utilized to distinguish a specific occasion.

In this way, let's make a couple occurrences to perceive how this functions:

Posting 15.2: Creating class occurrences

```
>>> x =  Hero ( )

>>> y = Hero ( )

>>>  z = Hero ( )
```

Here you'll see that bracket show up. This is to mean that these are occurrence articles made from the Hero class. Every one of these occurrences has literally the same properties, got from the Hero class. (Later on I'll demonstrate to you generally accepted methods to tweak a case to accomplish more than the base class).

Presently, lets include some data.

Posting 15.3: Adding information to examples

>>> x . setName (" Arthur , King o f the Brit-
ons ")

>>> y . setName (" S i r Lancelot , the Brave")

>>> z . setName (" S i r Robin , the Not–Quite–
So–Brave– As–Sir –Lancelot ")

These call the setName() technique that sits in
the Hero class. Nonetheless, as you probably are
aware at this point, everyone is for an alternate
occasion; not just do x, y, and z every have an alternate quality, however the first esteem in Hero
is left untouched.

On the off chance that you now call the show-
case() technique for every case, you ought to see
the name of every legend.

Posting 15.4: Displaying occurrence information

>>> x . d i s p l a y ( )

Arthur , King o f the Britons

>>> y . d i s p l a y ( )

S i r Lancelot , the Brave

```
>>> z . d i s p l a y ( )
```

S i r Robin , the Not–Quite–So–Brave–As–Sir
–Lancelot

You can change occurrence traits "on the fly" basically by appointing to self in routines inside the class protest or through expressly doling out to occasion objects.

Posting 15.5: Modifying occurrences

```
>>> x . name = " S i r Galahad , the Pure"
```

```
>>> x . d i s p l a y ( )
```

S i r Galahad , the Pure

That is sufficiently likely for this lesson. I'll cover whatever remains of classes in the following part yet this is ideally enough to give you a thought of how helpful classes and OOP all in all can be when programming. The lion's share of languages in current utilization actualize OOP to some degree, so figuring out how to utilize classes and articles will bail you out as you pick up learning.

Thankfully Python executes OOP in a sensible manner, so it's generally easy to learn in Python instead of something like C++, in any event as far as I can tell.

15.5 "New-style" classes

Beginning with Python 2.2, another sort of class was produced for Python. This new class gave an approach to programmers to make a class derived, straightforwardly or in a roundabout way, from an implicit Python sort, for example, a rundown, string, and so on.

You can make another class like the above cases, where no paren- proposition are utilized. Then again, you can likewise explicitly acquire your new class from the article class, or you can get another class from one of the inherent sorts. Posting 15.6 shows how this would look. Getting your custom classes from item is a smart thought, since Python 3.x just uses the "new-style" and precluding article can bring about issues. More information can be found at Introduction To New-Style Classes In Python and Python's New-style Classes.

Posting 15.6: New-style classes

class New Style User Defined Class (o b j e c t) :

pass

class Derived From Built In Type (l i s t) :

pass

class Indirectly Derived From Type (Derived From Built In Type) :

pass

15.6   A Note About Style

As said beforehand, Python has a certain "style-grammar" that is viewed as the "right" approach to compose Python programs. Zip 8 is the archive that depicts the greater part of the "endorsed" methods for composing. One of these is the way to recognize classes, capacities, strategies, and so forth.

Classes ought to be composed with the first letter promoted; any extra words in the class name ought to likewise be promoted: class SpamAndEggs(object). Capacities and routines ought to be composed in lower-case, with every word isolated by underscores: def bunny_vicious_bite().

Constants (variables that don't change quality) ought to be composed in all upper case: MAX_VALUE = 22.

There are numerous other complex thoughts to be worried about. I'll concede, I'm not the best about after Python's elaborate traditions but rather I attempt to tail them as well as can be expected recollect. Regardless of the possibility that I don't take after "the Python way", I do attempt to be steady inside I could call my own programs. My own proposal is to peruse PEP 8 and take a gander at the source code for distinctive Python programs, then pick a style that works best for you. The most essential thing is to maintain style.

CHAPTER SIXTEEN

MoreOOP

In the last chapter I told you some of the basics about using Python classes and object-oriented programming. It's time to delve more into classes and see how they make programming life better.

1.1   Inheritance

Most importantly, classes permit you to change a program without truly rolling out improvements to it. To expand, by subclassing a class, you can change the conduct of the program by essentially adding new parts to it instead of modifying the current segments.

As we've seen, an example of a class acquires the traits of that class. Then again, classes can likewise acquire properties from different classes. Consequently, a subclass acquires from a superclass permitting you to make a nonexclusive superclass that is specific through subclasses. The subclasses can override the rationale in a superclass, permitting you to change the conduct of your classes without changing the superclass by any means.

How about we make a basic illustration. In the first place make a class:

Posting 16.1: Defining a superclass

```
>>>c young lady F i r s t C l a s : #define the s u
p e r c l a s

... def s e t d a t a ( s e l f, esteem ): #define
techniques

...            s e l f . information = value
#' s e l f " r e f e r s to an occasion

... def d i s p l a y ( s e l f ):

...     print s e l f . information

...
```

At that point we make a subclass:

Posting 16.2: Defining a subclass

```
>>>c girl Second Class ( F i r s t C l a s ) :
#i n h e r i t s from Fi r s t Cl a s

...def d i s p l a y ( s e l f ) :      #r e d e f i n e s
"d i s p l a y "

...     print " Current esteem = '% s " % s e l f .
information

...
```

As should be obvious, SecondClass "overwrites" the presentation system. At the point when a FirstClass case is made, every last bit of its moves will be made from the systems characterized in FirstClass. At the point when a SecondClass case is made, it will utilize the acquired setdata() system from FirstClass however the showcase strategy will be the one from SecondClass.

To make this less demanding to see, here are a few cases in practice.

Posting 16.3: More legacy cases

```
>>>x=F i r s t C l a s ( ) #instance o f Fi r s t Cl
a s
```

```
>>>y=S econd Class ( ) #instance o f Second
Class

>>>x . s e t d a t a ( "The kid c a l e d Brian . " )

>>>y . s e t d a t a ( 42 )

>>>x . d i s p l a y ( )

The kid c a l e d Brian .

>>>y . d i s p l a y ( ) Current esteem = " 42 "
```

Both examples (x and y) utilize the same setdata() system from FirstClass; x utilizes it in light of the fact that it's an occasion of FirstClass while y utilizes it in light of the fact that SecondClass acquires setdata() from FirstClass. Notwithstanding, when the presentation system is called, x utilizes the definition from First- Class however y utilizes the definition from SecondClass, where showcase is overridden.

Since changes to program rationale can be made through subclasses, the utilization of classes for the most part backings code reuse and expansion better than customary capacities do. Capacities must be reworked to change how they function while classes can simply be subclassed to rethink techniques. On a last note, you can utilize numerous legacy (including more than one superclass inside of the enclosure) in the event that you require a class that has a place with distinctive gatherings. In principle this is great on the grounds that it ought to eliminate additional work. For instance, a man could be a culinary specialist, a musical artist, a store proprietor, and a programmer; the individual could acquire the properties from those parts. Be that as it may, truly it can be a genuine agony to deal with the different legacy sets. You need to ask yourself, "Is it truly important that this class acquire from these others?"; regularly the answer is, "No".

Utilizing various legacy is viewed as a "propelled system" and along these lines I won't examine it. Really, I don't utilize it; in the event that I experience a circumstance where I could utilize it, I attempt and reexamine the program's structure to abstain from utilizing it. It's sort of like normalizing databases; you continue separating it until it's as basic as you can get it. On the off chance that despite everything you require various legacy, then I prescribe getting a more propelled Python book.

16.2   Operator Overloads

Administrator over-burdening essentially implies that protests that you make from classes can react to activities (operations) that are as of now characterized inside of Python, for example, expansion, cutting, printing, and so on. Despite the fact that these activities can be actualized through class strategies, utilizing over-burdening binds the conduct closer to Python's article model and the item interfaces are more reliable to Python's inherent items, consequently over- stacking is simpler to learn and utilization.

Client made classes can override about the majority of Python's implicit operation systems. These routines are recognized by having two underlines prior and then afterward the technique name, similar to this: include . These methods are consequently called when Python assesses administrators; if a client class over-burdens the include technique, then when an expression has "+" in it, the client's system will be utilized rather than Python's implicit strategy.

Utilizing an illustration from the Learning Python book, here is the means by which administrator over-burdening would work practically speaking:

Posting 16.4: Operator over-burdening illustration

>>>c girl Third Class (Second Class) : #is −a Second Class

. . . def

__init__ (s e l f , esteem) :   #on " Third Class (

esteem)"

. . .   s e l f . information = esteem

. . . defadd   (s e l f , other) :   # on " s e l f + other "

. . . return Third Class (s e l f . information +

other)

...defmul (s e l f , other): #on " s e l f *
other "

...   s e l f . information = s e l f . information
* other

...

>>>a = Third Class (" abc ") #new

>>>a . d i s p l a y ( ) #i n h e r i t e d strategy

Current esteem = " abc "

__init__ c a l e d

>>>b = a + " xyz "#new add   c a l e d :
makes another example

>>>b . d i s p l a y ( )

Current esteem = " abcxyz "

>>>a *3   #new mul   c a l e d : changes
occasion in– p l pro

>>>a . d i s p l a y ( )

Current esteem = " abcabcabc "

ThirdClass is in fact a subclass of SecondClass however it doesn't override any of SecondClass' techniques. On the off chance that you needed, you could put the systems from ThirdClass in SecondClass and go from that point. How- steadily, making another subclass permits you adaptability in your program.

At the point when another example of ThirdClass is made, the init system takes the case creation contention and doles out it to self.data. Third- Class likewise overrides the "+" and "*" administrators; when one of these is experienced in an expression, the occasion question on the left of the administrator is gone to the self contention and the item on the privilege is gone to other. These strategies are unique in relation to the ordinary way Python manages "+" and "*" yet they just apply to examples of ThirdClass. Occasions of different classes still utilize the implicit Python techniques.

One last thing to say about administrator over-burdening is that you can make your custom strategies do whatever you need. In any case, basic practice is to take after the structure of the inherent techniques. That is, if an implicit system makes another article when called, your overriding strategy ought to as well. This lessens disarray when other individuals are utilizing your code. With respect to sample over, the constructed in strategy for determining "*" expressions makes another item (simply like how the "+" system does), accordingly the overriding technique we made ought to most likely make another protest as well, instead of changing the worth set up as it as of now does. You're not committed to "take after the tenets" but rather it does make life less demanding when things function not surprisingly.

16.3   Class Methods

Case systems (which is the thing that we've been utilizing in this way) and class techniques are the two approaches to call Python strategies. Point of fact, occasion techniques are naturally changed over into class routines by Python.

This is what I'm discussing. Let's assume you have a class:

Posting 16.5: Class techniques, section 1

```
class P r i n t C l a s :

def print Method ( s e l f , info ) :

print info
```

Presently we'll call the class' technique utilizing the ordinary example system and the "new" class strategy:

Posting 16.6: Class techniques, section 2

```
>>>x = P r i n t C l a s ( )

>>>x . print Method ( " Try spam ! " ) #instance
technique

Attempt spam !

>>>P r i n t C l a s . print Method ( x , "Purchase
more spam ! " )      # c l a s technique

Purchase  more  spam !
```

Anyway, what is the advantage of utilizing class

systems? All things considered, when utilizing legacy you can augment, as opposed to supplant, acquired conduct by calling a system through the class instead of the occurrence.

Here's a nonexclusive sample:

Posting 16.7: Class techniques and legacy

```
>>>c young lady  Super :

...     def strategy ( s e l f ) :

...     print "now in  Super . strategy"

...

>>>c girl  S ub c l a s ( Super ) :

...     def strategy ( s e l f ) :      #override system

...             print " s t a r t i n g  S ub c l a s . method"      # new activities

...     Super . strategy ( s e l f )   #d e f a u l t activity

...     print " finishing  Su b c l a s . strategy"
```

. . .

>>>x = Super ( )   #make a Super occurrence

>>>x . strategy ( )   #run Super . system

presently in Super . strategy

>>>x = S ub c l a s ( )   #make a Subclass occurrence

>>>x . strategy ( )   #run Subclass . system which c a l s Super . technique

s t a r t i n g S u bc l as s . strategy now in Super . system finishing S ub c l a s . technique

Utilizing class routines thusly, you can have a subclass expand the default system activities by having specific subclass activities yet still call the first default conduct through the superclass. By and by, I haven't utilized this yet however it is decent to realize that its accessible if required.

1.1   Have you seen myclass?

There is more to classes than I have covered here but I think I've covered most of the basics. Hopefully you have enough knowledge to use them; the more you work with them the easier they are to figure out. I may have mentioned it before, but it took meal most six months to get my head around using classes. Objects were a new area for me and I couldn't figure out how everything worked. It didn't help that my first exposure to them was Java and C++; my two textbooks just jumped right into using objects and classes without explaining the

how ' s and why's of them. I hope I did better explaining them than my text books did.

There are several "gotchas" when using classes, such as learning the difference between "is-a" and "has-a" relationships, but most of them are pretty obvious, especially when you get error messages. If you really get stumped, don't be afraid to ask questions. Remember, we were all beginners once and so many of us have encountered the same problem before.

CHAPTER SEVENTEEN

DATABASES

Data bases are popular for many applications, especially for use with web applications or customer-oriented programs. There is a cave although; data bases don't have the performance that file-system based applications do.

Normal files, such as text files, are easy to create and use; Python has the tools built-in and it doesn't take much to work with files. File systems are more efficient (most of the time) in terms of performance because you don't have the over head of data base queries or other things to worry about. And files are easily portable between operating systems (assuming you aren't using appropriately format) and are often editable/ usable with different programs.

Data bases are good when discrete "structures" are to be operated on, e.g. a customer list that has

phone numbers, addresses, past orders, etc. Ada-
tabasecanstorealumpofdataandallowtheuserorde-
velopertopullthenecessaryinformation, without
regard to how the data Is stored. Additionally, data
bases can be used to retrieved at a randomly, rather than sequentially. For pure sequential process-
ing, a standard file is better.

Obviously, there is more to the file-system vs. data
base battle than what I just covered. But, generally speaking, you will be better suit educing a
file-system structure than a data base unless there
is a reason to use a data base. My personal recom-
mendation is that, unless you are creating a serv-
er-based application, try using a local file rather
than a data base. If that doesn't work, then you
can try a data base.

1.1   How to Use a Database

A data base (DB) is simply a collect ion of data,
place din to an arbitrary structured format. The
most common DB is relational data base; tables
are used to store the data and relationships can be
defined between different tables. SQL (Structured

Query Language) is the language used to work with most DBs. (SQL can either be pronounced as discrete letters "S-Q-L" or as a word "sequel". I personally use "sequel".)

SQL provides the commands to query a data base and retrieve or manipulate information. The format of a query is one of the most powerful forces when working with DBs; an improper query won't return the desire din formation, or worse, it will return the wrong information. SQL is also used to input information in to a DB.

While you can interact directly with a DB using SQL, as a programmer have the liberty of using Python to control much of the interactions. You will still have to know SQL so you can populate and interact with the DB, but most of the calls to the DB will be with the Python DB-API (data base application programming interface).

1.2   Working With a Database

This book is not intended to be a data base or SQL primer. However, I will provide you with enough information to create simple data base and an application that uses it. First, I will cover the basic principles of databases and SQL queries then we will use Python to make and manipulate as mall database.

First off, consider a database to be one or more tables, just like a spreadsheet. The vertical columns comprise different fields or categories; they are analogous to the fields you fill out in a form. The horizontal rows are individual records; each row is one complete record entry. Here's a pictorial summary, representing a customer list. The table's name is "Customers_table":

Index	Last_Name	First_Name	Address	City	State
0	Johnson	Jack	123EasySt.	Any-where	CA
1	Smith	John	312HardSt.	Some-where	NY

The only column that needs special explanation is the Index field. This field isn't required but is highly recommended. You can name it anything you want but the purpose is the same. It is a field that provides a unique value to every record; it's often called the primary key field. The primary key is a special object for most databases; simply identifying which field is the primary key will automatically increment that field as new entries are made, thereby ensuring a unique data object for easy identification. The other fields are simply created based on the information that you want to include in the database.

To make a true relational database, you have one table that refers to one or more tables in some fashion. If I wanted to make a order-entry database, I could make another table that tracks an order and relate that order to the above customer list, likeso:

Key	Item_title	Price	Order_Number	Customer_ID
0	Boots	55.50	4455	0
1	Shirt	16.00	4455	0
2	Pants	33.00	7690	0
3	Shoes	23.99	3490	1
4	Shoes	65.00	5512	1

This table is called "Orders_table". This table shows the various orders made by each person in the customer table. Each entry has a unique key and is related to Customers_table by the Customer_ID field, which is the Index value for each customer.

17.3   Using SQL to Query a Database

To inquiry a table utilizing SQL, you essentially tell the database what it is you are attempting to do. On the off chance that you need to get a rundown of the clients or a rundown of requests in the system, simply select what parts of the table you need to get. (Note: the accompanying code bits are not Python particular; also, SQL articulations are not case-delicate but rather are generally composed in uppercase for clarity.)

Posting 17.1: Returning information with SQL

SELECT * FROM Customers_ table

The outcome ought to pretty look simply like the table over; the command just pulls everything from Customers_table and prints it. The printed results may be text based or have network lines; contingent upon nature you are utilizing yet the data will all be there.

You can likewise restrict the choice to particular fields, for example,

Posting 17.2: Limiting results with SQL

SELECT Last_name , First_name FROM Customers_ table

SELECT Address FROM Customers_ table WHERE State == "NY"

The second SQL question above uses the "WHERE" articulation, which gives back a restricted arrangement of data taking into account the condition indicated. In the event that you utilized the announcement as thought of, you ought to just get back the locations of clients who live in New York State. Clearly this is a smart thought in light of the fact that it confines the outcomes you need to process and it diminishes the measure of memory being utilized. Numerous system stoppages can be followed to awful DB questions that arrival a lot of data and devour an excess of assets.

To join the data from two tables, i.e. to tackle the force of social databases, you need to join the tables in the question.

Posting 17.3: Joining database tables

SELECT Last_name , First_name , Order_ Number FROM Customers_table , Orders_ table WHERE Customers_ table . File = Orders_ table

.

Customer_ID

This ought to give you something that resembles this:

Posting 17.4: SQL inquiry results Johnson Jack 4455

Johnson Jack 4455

Johnson Jack 7690

Smith John 3490

Smith John 5512

Once more, the arranging may be diverse relying upon the system you are working with however it's the data that matters.

17.4 Python and SQLite

Beginning with v2.5, Python has included SQLite, a light-weight SQL library. SQLite is composed in C, so it's fast. It likewise makes the database in a solitary record, which makes actualizing a DB genuinely basic; you don't need to stress over all the issues of having a DB spread over a server. In any case, it improves suited to either improvement purposes or little, remain solitary applications. In the event that you are anticipating utilizing your Python program for expansive scale systems, you'll need to move to a more powerful database, for example, PostgreSQL or MySQL.

In any case, this doesn't mean SQLite isn't helpful. It's useful for genius to begin typing your application before you toss in an all out DB; that way you know your program meets expectations and any issues are in all likelihood with the DB execution. It's likewise useful for little programs that needn't bother with a complete DB bundle with its related overhead.

Anyway, how would you utilize SQLite with Python? I'll demonstrate to you.

17.5   Creating a SQLite DB

Since SQLite is incorporated with Python, you just import it like some other library. Once foreign made, you need to make an association with it; this makes the database record. A cursor is the article inside SQLite that performs a large portion of the capacities you will be doing with the DB.

Posting 17.5: Creating a SQLite database

```
import sqlite3   #SQLite v3 is the adaptation curently included with Python

association = sqlite3.unite(" Hand_tools.db")   #

The .db expansion is optional

cursor = association.cursor()

#Alternative DB made just in memory
```

```
#mem_conn = s q l i t e 3 . unite ( " : memory : " )

#cursor = mem_conn. cursor ( )

c u r s o r . execute ( """CREATE TABLE  Tools

( i d  INTEGER PRIMARY KEY,

name TEXT, s i z e  TEXT,

cost  INTEGER) """ )

for  thing  in  (

( None ,  " Knife " ,  " Small " ,  15 ) ,          #The
end comma i s  obliged  to  separate  t u p l e  i
tems

( None ,  " Machete" ,  "Medium" ,  35 ) ,

( None ,  "Hatchet" ,  " Large " ,  55 ) ,

( None ,  " Hatchet " ,  " Small " ,  25 ) ,

( None , "Mallet" , " Small " , 25 )

( None , " Screwdriver " , " Small " , 10 ) ,

( None ,  " Prybar " ,  " Large " ,  60 ) ,

) : c u r s o r . execute ( "Supplement  INTO  Tools
```

```
VALUES ( ? ,

? , ? , ?) " , thing )

association . submit ( )      #Write  information
to  database

c u r s o r . c l o s e ( )      #Close  database
```

The above code makes a straightforward, single-table database of a collection of hand instruments. Notice the question marks used to embed things into the table. The question marks are utilized to keep a SQL infusion assault, where a SQL order is gone to the DB as a honest to goodness esteem. The DB program will prepare the summon as an ordinary, legitimate charge which could erase information, change information, or generally bargain your DB. The question marks go about as a substitution worth to keep this from happening.

You'll likewise take note of the capacity to make a DB in memory. This is useful for testing, when you would prefer not to take the time to keep in touch with circle or stress over indexes. On the off chance that you have enough memory, you can likewise make the DB totally in memory for your last item; on the other hand, on the off chance that you lose force or generally have memory issues, you lose the complete DB. I just utilize a RAM DB when I'm trying the introductory execution to verify I have the language structure and arrangement right. When I check it meets expectations the way I need, then I transform it to make a plate based DB.

17.6   Pulling Data from a DB

To recover the information from a SQLite DB, you simply utilize the SQL commands that tell the DB what data you need and how you need it arrange

Listing17.6: Retrieving data from SQLite

```
cursor.execute("SELECT name, size, price
FROM Tools")toolsTuple = cursor.fetchall()
fortuple intoolsTuple:
    name, size, price = tuple      #un-
    packthetuplesitem= ("%s, %s, %d"%
    (name, size, price ))printitem
```

Whichreturnsthefollowinglist:

Listing17.7:Re-
turneddataKnife, Small, 15

Machete, Medium, 35

Axe, Large, 55Hatchet, Small, 25Hammer,
Small, 25

Screwdriver, Small, 10Prybar, Large,
60Knife, Small, 15Machete, Medium, 35Axe,
Large, 55

Hatchet, Small, 25Hammer, Small,
25Screwdriver, Small, 10Prybar, Large, 60

Alternatively,ifyouwanttoprintoutpretty-
tables,youcandosomethinglikethis:

Listing17.8:"Prettyprinting"returneddatacursor.
execute("SELECT *FROM Tools")

forrow**in**cursor:

> **print**"-"* 10

print"ID:", row[0]

print"Name:", row[1]

print"Size:", row[2]**print**"Price:", row[3]
print"–"* 10

Whichgivesyouthis:

Listing17.9:Outputof"prettyprinted"-
data

––––––––––––

ID: 1

Name:KnifeSize:SmallPrice: 15

––––––––––

––––––––––

ID: 2

Name: MacheteSize: MediumPrice: 35

––––––––––

––––––––––

ID: 3

Name: Axe

Size: LargePrice: 55

———————

———————

ID: 4

Name: HatchetSize: Small

Price: 25

———————

———————

ID: 5

Name:HammerSize: SmallPrice: 25

———————

———————

ID: 6

Name:ScrewdriverSize: Small

Price: 10

_____

_____

ID: 7

Name: PrybarSize: LargePrice: 60

_____

_____

ID: 8

Name:KnifeSize:SmallPrice: 15

_____

_____

ID: 9

Name: MacheteSize: MediumPrice: 35

_____

_____

ID: 10

Name: Axe

Size: LargePrice: 55

———————

———————

ID: 11

Name: HatchetSize: Small

Price: 25

———————

———————

ID: 12

Name:HammerSize: SmallPrice: 25

———————

———————

ID: 13

Name:ScrewdriverSize: Small

Price: 10

ID: 14

Name: PrybarSize: LargePrice: 60

Obviously, you can mess around with the formatting to present the information as you desire, such as giving columns with headers, including or removing certain fields,etc.

1.3   SQLite Database Files

SQLite will try to recreate the database file every time you run the program. If the DB file already exists, you will get an "OperationalError" exception stating that the file already exists. The easiest way to deal with this is to simply catch the exception and ignore it try:

Listing17.10: Dealing with existing databases

```
cursor.execute("CREATETABLEFoo(idIN-
```

TEGERPRIMARYKEY,nameTEXT)")**except**
sqlite3.Operational Error: pass

This will allow you to run your database program
multiple times (such as during creation or testing)
without having to delete the DBfile after every run.
You can also use a similar try/except block when
testing to see if the DBfile already exists; if the file
doesn't exist, then you can call the DB creation
module. This allows you to put the DB creation
code in a separate module from your "core" program, calling it only when needed executes in a
single Python step, and is, therefore, thread safe.

www.ingramcontent.com/pod-product-compliance
Lightning Source LLC
Chambersburg PA
CBHW071417050326
40689CB00010B/1874